RISING TIDES REVISITED
The Loss of Coastal Heritage in Orkney

RISING TIDES REVISITED
The Loss of Coastal Heritage in Orkney

Photos: *Frank Bradford*
Text: *Julie Gibson*

This book is dedicated to the memory of Judith Robertson.

First published by Northings, 2008.
This edition published in 2012 by Orkney Archaeology Society.

ISBN 978-0-9573379-0-9

Copyright © Julie Gibson & Frank Bradford, 2008 and 2012.

All rights reserved.
No part of this publication may be reproduced, stored in a retrieval system or transmitted, in any form, by any means, electronic, mechanical, photocopying, recording or otherwise, with the prior written permission of the publishers.

A CIP catalogue record for this book is available from the British Library.

Printed by
The Shetland Times Ltd.,
Gremista, Lerwick, Shetland,
ZE1 0PX, Scotland.

This intricately decorated brooch is one part of the grave goods discovered in the pagan Viking boat grave at Scar on the north coast of Sanday. The grave was dug for a rich elderly lady and her grave companions, a man and teenager. Similar "Troms type equal arm" brooches are overwhelmingly found in Northern Norway. The goods within the grave were all antique when they were buried at about 1000 AD. Most harked back to Norway. The whale bone plaque (see cover) that was buried with it also probably originated there. Even the sand in the caulking of the boat was Norwegian. The people who buried the Scar lady were making a point about her pagan Norwegian roots. Perhaps they found it particularly important to assert her identity in the face of burgeoning Christianity. The point is, that roots are important — they were important then and they are important today. Nearly half the grave had gone before it was discovered and excavated. NGR HY 678 458.

Contents

Introduction 9
  Climate change and sea-levels 9
  The significance of the damage to archaeology 10
  Site Selection 11
  Access and safety 12
  Do's and Dont's 12

South Ronaldsay and Burray 13
  Kirkhoose, Widewall Bay, South Ronaldsay 14
  St Ola's chapel, Kirkhoose, Widewall Bay, South Ronaldsay 15
  Kirkhoose, Widewall Bay, South Ronaldsay 16
  Castle of Burwick 17
  East Broch, Burray 18

Deerness 22
  The Brough of Deerness 23
  Hogback grave stone, Skaill, Deerness 26
  Skaill, Deerness 27

West Mainland 28
  Breckness, Stromness 29
  Broch of Borwick, Sandwick 30

Rousay 31
  Midhowe broch, Rousay 32
  Viera Lodge broch, Rousay 33
  Gateway to the Atlantic Project at Swandro 34

Eday 35
  Calf of Eday, Salt Works 36
  Calf of Eday, chambered cairns 37
  Maltbarn, Eday 38

Stronsay 39
  The Danes Pier, Stronsay 40
  Lamb Head broch, Stronsay 41
  Tams Castle, Stronsay 42
  Ward of Housebay, Stronsay 43

Westray 44
  Knowe of Skea, The Mortuary House 46
  Knowe of Skea, Berstness, Westray 47
  Knowe of Skea, Berstness, Westray 49

Links of Noltland, Westray 50
Westray Wife, Links of Noltland, Westray 52
Cross Kirk, Tuquoy, Westray 53
Tuquoy, Westray 54
Castle of Burrian, Westray 56
Evertaft, Westray 57
Hodgalee, broch, Westray 58
Hodgalee, Iron-age buildings, Westray 59
Hodgalee, Westray 60
Hodgalee, Westray 61
Quoygrew, Westray 62
Quoygrew, Westray 63
Trenabie and Quoygrew, Westray 64
Knowe of Burristae, Westray 65
Burristae, Westray 66
Pierowall Westray 67

Papa Westray 69
  St Boniface and Munkerhoose, Papa Westray 70
  Munkerhoose and St Boniface, Papa Westray 71
  Munkerhoose and St Boniface, Papa Westray 72
  Knap of Howar, Papa Westray 73
  Knap of Howar, Papa Westray 74
  Weelies Taing, Papa Westray 75

Sanday 79
  Tofts, Sanday 81
  Newark, Sanday 82
  Fish Trap at Newark, Sanday 84
  Stove Farm, Sanday 85
  Stove Bay Neolithic Site, Sanday 86
  Burnt Mound, Meur, Sanday 88
  Tresness chambered cairn, Sanday 89
  Tresness chambered cairn, Sanday 90
  Northskaill farm mound, Sanday 91
  B98, Bay of Lopness, Sanday 92

North Ronaldsay 93
  Broch of Burrian, North Ronaldsay 94
  Broch of Burrian finds, North Ronaldsay 96

Dennis Head Lighthouse, North Ronaldsay 97
Lighthouse pier 98
The Sheep-dyke, North Ronaldsay 99
Shapinsay 101
Odin's Stone, Shapinsay 102
The Hillock, Shapinsay 103
Galtness and Castle Batteries, Shapinsay 104
Broch of Steiro, Shapinsay 105
Hoy & Waas 107
Walls Battery 108
Walls Battery 109
Graffitti at Walls Battery 110
Brims 111
The Skeo 112
Prehistoric Landscape near Skipi Geo 113
Crockness Martello Tower 114
Timeline for coast watchers: 115
Mesolithic - about 8,000 years ago: 115
Neolithic period c. 3,500 BC to c.2,000 BC 115
The Bronze Age about 1800 BC to about 500BC 116
Iron Age, Pictish & Viking Age. About 500BC to 1065AD 117
Medieval and modern 119

Further Reading and information sites: 120

Orkney Archaeology Society 122

Inundation of St Margaret's Hope January 12th 2005. Scenes like this will become more common due to climate change.

Introduction

This book was created as a collection of photos of some of Orkney's coastal archaeology. It is an introduction to an amazingly rich resource that opens up the histories of 6 millennia of people in Orkney and yet has very little future. There is quite an idiosyncratic selection of coastal sites included here, ranging from the sublime, such as the tumbling walls of Hodgalee, to the ridiculous – an apparently very ordinary rock grandiosely named Odin's Stone. There has been no attempt at covering everything, or getting into all districts. Westray is better served than most areas, but even so, there is a lot more to be seen in that island. On the way to the sites in this book, you will undoubtedly discover others. Most of the archaeology is off the beaten track, it is raw, it is ruinous and, impossible as it seems when you look at the solid walls in some of these sites, the sea can take them in a single tide. Some sites will not be here for very long. You are recommended to go out and visit them now.

Climate change and sea-levels

The last ice age in mainland Scotland peaked about 18,000 years ago when much of the country was covered in ice, some of it up to a kilometre thick. Glaciers crawled across the landscape gouging out broad valleys, and depositing clay on the rocks beneath. This ice was incredibly heavy and depressed the earth's surface beneath. When the ice retreated two things happened together: as ice melted the sea level rose, and once the downward pressure of all that ice on the land was removed, the land rebounded, also rising. Whether or not land drowns, or by contrast rises out of the sea depends on the local relationship between the speeds of both movements.

Rebound happens at its fastest as the ice releases its grip and is related to the weight of ice. In Orkney it is thought that there was perhaps only half as much ice as that which covered the Highlands of Scotland, and it was gone earlier. Therefore the isostatic rebound of land following the melting of the glaciers over Orkney is now slower than that of the Highlands. This leaves the Highlands still gradually rising in relation to the sea, but in Orkney the sea is slowly gaining.

In the absence of hard data, "guestimates" were that the sea has risen an average of a metre for each thousand years over the last 8,000 years subdividing islands and inundating low lying lochs with sea water. It is thus possible for instance that Westray, Papa Westray and the Holm of Papay were one island as recently as the Neolithic period. We are just beginning to acquire some dating evidence at least for the more recent millennia: It has for long been known that some bays round Orkney contain peat which was formed on land prior to being inundated. At Otterswick in Sanday, tree stumps in the peat have recently been dated to the beginning of the Neolithic period, some 6,500 years ago and it can be seen that sea levels have risen about 3 metres since. A rate of half a metre per millennium.

It is of course not so simple a story. At intervals through time, the sea has thrown up sand which has also blown up onto the land. At times this has been a gradual, probably annual event and people have still managed to work it. At other times, some even quite recent, when great sand movement occurred, it infilled bays and covered agricultural land, making it impossible to till. It is thought that a catastrophic sand-blow may have been what caused the Neolithic village of Skara Brae to be abandoned. But that village was preserved by the blanketing sand that supported stonework and created a good chemical environment for the preservation of bone. This type of environment applies to substantial areas of Orkney – and is one of the reasons why the archaeological record here is so particularly good. But being coastal and sandy it is also soft and particularly threatened by destruction through storms.

Nowadays there is anxiety over the melting of the ice over Greenland and Antartica and the many smaller glaciers. Scientific debates as to how much will melt, whether or not there is or will be a net increase in sea-level due to this, or whether increased precipitation in the form of more snow may counteract the melt by locking up the water, continue. But the overall increase in sea levels in the past century or so does seem to have been concentrated in the last 20 years, and it would seem reasonable to assume that this may be the start of a trend due to global warming. This is bad news for the vulnerable coasts of Scotland.

Predictions of future sea levels for Orkney vary. In part this is because very little data has been gathered about the past, on which to build scientific models. Research into changing sea levels and climate has led to predictions for Orkney of a 30cm rise in sea levels over the next 100 years. If the sea were calm, sea level rise would not be so troublesome. A sea wall or two would do the trick. (New Orleans was alright until the wind blew!) But the increase in storminess and wave height which is also occurring has led to some serious discussion about giant "50 year" waves forming more often. It has been observed that wave heights at the Schiehallion oil platform to the West of Shetland have been increasing: some have measured 25m from crest to base. Whereas Orkney lies well to the south-east, waves and storm surges have done lot of damage to Orkney's archaeology and threaten parts of Kirkwall and many of the rural low-lying settlements inhabited today. (For references to this and further reading see Tom Dawson (Ed) 2003, Coastal Archaeology and Erosion in Scotland, available on the web.)

The significance of the damage to archaeology

Orcadian identity has been formed by Orkney's people, living and working in its landscapes and seascapes through time. For most of our human past there is no source of information but what is available through the study of its material remains- archaeology. In historical times the archaeological record has a story to tell of individuals or actions perhaps too commonplace to merit a place in the history books. The skeletal remains of our ancestors, our buildings, rubbish dumps, soils, landscapes, and the changes wrought during millennia are sources that enable the understanding of that identity.

Orkney's archaeological resource is of national and international importance – our prehistoric archaeology with its all round great preservation is impossible to match in other areas of Northern Europe. Orkney's place in the centre of a maritime world stretching from the North Sea to the North Atlantic is attested by cultural connections linking Orkney at different times to Brittany, Greenland, Tromso or the Low Countries. Was the architecture of Orcadian Neolithic society the inspiration for that of Stonehenge? The Inscription of some our sites in the West Mainland in the list of World Heritage Sites is recognition of the quality of our archaeological heritage.

Scotland is a sea-faring, coastal nation. The archaeology of Orkney reflects this. The archipelago is made up of many small islands. People have been here for at least seven or eight thousand years, and each generation has lived their lives in relation to the sea, as well as the land. Of these sites, many relate to the stories of Orcadians as islanders. They are monuments to how we interacted with the sea. Piers, jetties, sea dykes, fish traps, stone quarries, all existed in the land between the tides. Fish houses, nousts, and light houses are in specifically coastal locations. One of the smaller islands, North Ronaldsay, has its own story to tell through its encircling dyke, of pressure for land. But not only are these specific types of site under threat – every land-based type of site is threatened and being damaged too, farms from all periods, prehistoric tombs, graveyards and churches, gardens, fields, and even the remains of woodland.

There are hundreds of sea-damaged or threatened sites and monuments on the coast. In a survey conducted a decade ago of very roughly one third of the coast, 843 sites were found to be threatened. A conservative estimate based upon this and allowing for thinner distribution of sites on inhospitable cliffs would be that we have in excess of 1,700 sites on the brink. This would constitute approximately half of the known sites of Orkney. It is a highly alarming proportion of our main resource for understanding past peoples and societies, and Orkney's place in the world.

In Orkney it is not just our understanding or feeling for our roots which is threatened by the piecemeal removal of the sites, archaeology provides the fundamental part of our infrastructure for tourism. Except in Hoy, we do not have "sublime" Highland mountainous landscapes, we do not have many castles or great houses or botanic gardens. But instead we have an accessible, often three dimensional, archaeological resource that allows visitors the feeling of inhabiting the past. And this brings in a lot of money and creates a lot of jobs. Surveys have demonstrated a quarter of our visitors are drawn to Orkney by our archaeology.

Although coastal damage and destruction can be seen to be inevitable, it can be slowed to the point where a hard-nosed economic case can be made for protecting individual sites. Investment in business rarely has a forward plan for centuries, and nor should this be necessary when planning to invest in archaeology. Skara Brae, our Neolithic village that is at the heart of the tourism industry, will eventually be destroyed by the sea. But it has already been around as a visitor attraction (albeit requiring sea-wall, maintenance and loving care) for more than half a century. The government investment made in Gordon Childe's archaeological work in the 1920's to clear it out and each subsequent investment has paid off in economic terms for Orkney and for Scotland many times over. The privately owned Tomb of the Eagles is the result of one family's enterprising commitment to excavating and conserving an eroding Neolithic cliff-top tomb. These two sites have created for visitors coming from everywhere in the world to Orkney an unforgettable experience of intimate encounters with Stone Age people. The current and long-term lack of investment in archaeology at national levels is short-sighted, and is leading to a permanent reduction in development potential.

Site Selection

For this book I left out most of the famous sites, even where they are on the coast. Next, I chose my favourites, but only those with reasonably easy access. Then some were picked to illustrate the extraordinarily rich variety of sites and one or two photos were added of the finds that lay within them. We did make one or two exceptions to the access criterion and included for instance the Calf of Eday salt-works which requires a dinghy hire to get there. For which calm weather is a requirement. But I reckon that this site alone justifies the trip across Calf Sound (and you get two chambered cairns and an Iron Age house, not illustrated, on an uninhabited island, and an all round great experience, thrown in for free).

The photos were taken between 2006 and 2007. It is probably true that your view of any site is going to be a one-off. And it will be different again the following year. Parts of the site will go, and new details will be exposed. This makes each visit a voyage of discovery. You will find walls and floors, middens consisting of soils, ash and food debris, pottery and stone tools. The random way that the sea can take elements of the site and leave others does not often help with understanding what is present! You may wish to record or monitor sites yourself: Take photos with at least a general view and close-ups of detail and please note where you are! A map reference is vital. Let the County Archaeologist know about your observations.

Access and Safety

Most of the sites featured are got to by walking and scrambling along the beach, occasionally resorting to the grassy tops of the shore banks. Most are not publicly displayed, some are on more "official" paths or routes, but most are not. There is a right to roam in most places in Scotland. Nevertheless it is important to stay safe and to be considerate. Scottish Natural Heritage publishes guidance. I offer some handy hints in addition that are mostly common sense. Real car parks are rare. It is important to ensure that wherever you leave your car you don't block gateways or tracks etc. but leave space for a giant tractor and trailer to get past you. Check out the long grass for hidden ditches: this is best done before you need to find a tractor to tow you out! Obviously don't park up in fields or farmyards and don't go into people's farmyards or gardens, unless specifically invited. Leave gates as you find them.

You should be wary of walking on your own and it is much safer to walk with a companion. It is very easy to fall. If you are on your own, take the precaution of letting someone know when you are due back and where you are going. Check out the mobile phone coverage, and take one with you. Take care whilst walking, and use a stick if you feel uncertain about walking on rough or slippery ground. The shore is not an entirely safe place. If you see green slime on shelving flat rocks on the shore, avoid it because it is as slippery as ice. Beware of the tide coming in and trapping you. Crossings to tidal islands can be very dodgy when the water is on them: it is essential you check your tide times and get advice locally and only cross when safe.

The weather in Orkney is extremely changeable. At most times of year you will get cold if you stay still, unless well dressed. It is important to wear many layers and take a wind and waterproof top and trousers with you on most days. A hat is usually needed. Ironically, even when the wind is taking away all the heat, there is still the chance that when the sun shines you can get sunburnt on those bits that are exposed. Ladies Beware! The creation of a highly unattractive "farmers tan" will result unless sun-blocked! You should consider taking water with you. Frightening beasts include birds, cattle and midges! Cattle can be seriously dangerous, and dogs and stock do not mix.

The archaeology you will encounter is for the most part falling down and out. Common sense will mean that you do not stand under it. But sometimes, as in the case of most wartime archaeology, it is positively dangerous. For instance, glass windows can explode out of their frames without warning. Concrete reinforced by, or laid onto metal is liable to collapse. Holes, pits, underground tanks and trenches are everywhere.

Do's and Don't's

It is absolutely essential to treat the sites with respect – and do like the safari guides say and take only photos. Apart from the fact that looting and damaging sites is unethical, many sites are Scheduled Ancient Monuments which means that it is illegal to damage them, or to alter them in any way without permission. In Scotland, any ancient object that is found must by law be reported to the museum for the consideration of treasure-troving. Human remains should not be removed or disturbed, and must be reported to the police, museum or archaeologist. If you wish to help and contribute to keeping an eye on the recession of sites, all pieces of information will be gratefully received. Meanwhile a selection of the best "wild" archaeology you are ever likely to encounter follows. It's an endangered species.

South Ronaldsay and Burray

Kirkhoose, Widewall Bay, South Ronaldsay

It is not known how much of this site remains, but it is the first Viking site to be confirmed in this particular island, discovered only in the last couple of years. It would no doubt repay further investigation. Here we have a sheltered bay in which a boat could be anchored and landed, good rich farmland and a running stream. This is perfect territory for the incoming Norse colonists. NGR HY 434 914.

Previous page:

The Tomb of the Eagles together with its visitor centre provides the opportunity for close encounters with the people of the Neolithic in Orkney. The story of this cliff-edge monument's excavation and conservation by Ronnie Simison is inspirational.

St Ola's chapel, Kirkhoose, Widewall Bay, South Ronaldsay

In this spooky corner of the inner end of Widewall Bay, skeletons were found eroding out of the shingle. These are the ribs that first drew the attention of an eagle-eyed member of the public. They are hard to make out even in the photograph, having been very abraded by the sea. Other small amounts of various human bones were found on the beach nearby. The records show that a chapel once existed down near the shore but the exact location is forgotten.

The old farm nearby takes its name from its associations with the chapel itself, but the connections are even closer. The soil from the graveyard at the shore is said to have been taken to improve the gardens of the farm in the 19th century. There are many ghost stories associated with the house which once, allegedly, had a gibbet on one end that was used for summary justice following conviction in the court room within.

Now the erosion at the coast has revealed low red sandstone foundations with lime mortar. These are likely to be part of what remains of the chapel. And moving south east along the shore we pass the site of the graves and come to a low earthy cliff section containing middens, burnt stones, wall foundations and flagged floor surfaces. Fragments of soapstone vessel were discovered in the shore face and the stones of the beach. They included parts of round bottomed bowls, likely to have been made in Norway, and brought with the first Viking colonists. Other Norwegian connections are made through the dedication of the chapel to St Olaf, the Norwegian king and saint.

Kirkhoose, Widewall Bay, South Ronaldsay

The red sandstone blocks in the foreground are probably the remains of St Ola's (Olaf's) chapel. Behind, an archaeologist is working to lift and record the eroding skeleton. Below this grave was another with the skull protected by a stone "head box", an arrangement of three stones on edge and a small lid. This is a style of Christian burial that is known (from burials discovered next to Skaill House, Sandwick) to have been practised in Orkney in the 14th century.

Castle of Burwick

Danger! The remains pictured below are sixty feet up on a very dangerous stack site. You can see in the centre of the picture a cleft in the cliff into which turf is falling. This split runs horizontally for a good distance into the stack itself, and is of unknown depth. This fissure is overgrown by matted grass at the surface. You could easily lose your life visiting this site. You are strongly advised to stick to the path on the cliff top and do not venture out beyond.

When standing on the path (HY ND 435 843) you can see the turf covered remains (not pictured) of what may be a medieval castle site. The evidence for this is its squared shape, broad dimensions and its position overlooking the Pentland Firth. Without the ability to look below the long grass and into the natural lie of the land, it's hard to say for certain but the "castle" does seem to be stratigraphically superimposed upon what may be prehistoric buildings beneath. These are created from dry stone walling incorporating upright slabs set at right angles.

The date and use of this 4cm long bronze item has not yet been identified. It was found here exposed on a piece of paving and could have dropped out of any of the layers of occupation nearby. If I had to guess (which in this case I do!) I would say this site has Iron Age roots, but a medieval re-occupation starting back in the 11th century. Banks and ditches cut the peninsular off from the land.

East Broch, Burray

This broch is a fine memorial to the excavators Petrie and Farrer who were a prolific Orcadian antiquarian double-act of the mid 19th century. They became great when they collaborated with Sir Henry Dryden an architect and surveyor who illustrated some of their excavations. Dryden added surveyed plans to Petrie's notes. (Farrer was not so keen on the paperwork!) George Petrie worked as factor or estates manager of the Graemeshall Estate and Farrer was a major landowner of the time, who encouraged Petrie in his excavations. They are most famous for Petrie's work at Maes Howe Neolithic tomb.

Invisible hazards lurk at some of our sites. Just outside the entrance was an underground chamber, running roughly north to south. Nine steps led down to what was described as a rock cut chamber deep below. It contained a quern stone. These so-called earth houses are one of the features of the later Bronze Age and Iron Age. They appear mostly in association with dwellings, and their purpose or meaning is not yet understood. For some years consideration was given to their being places of refuge, or food storage. Now those ideas are giving way to the proposal that these are spiritual places. Few archaeological sites (and probably none that are featured in this book) are entirely safe, what with loose ankle breaking stones, and the potential for chambers to collapse. So you should take care.

East Broch, Burray

The clay banks of this broch are an unusual feature. Although it is common, or most usual, for a broch to be enclosed, they are usually surrounded by ditches as well as banks, and sometimes walls. Here there is no sign of a ditch and the clay is heaped high. The technique of scraping and mounding clay was often employed in the creation of burial mounds in the Bronze Age. It is clear that some brochs are built on earlier features. It is possible therefore that these clay banks were created in the Bronze Age and the broch was built within what was an already significant space.

Next page: The block ship pictured was sunk in World War I to prevent incursions of German vessels into the British naval anchorage of Scapa Flow.

Deerness

The Brough of Deerness

Park up near The Gloup that is a large and sinister hole in the ground, filled with waves, and walk out along the cliff top to the stack site called the Brough of Deerness. It will take you maybe a quarter of an hour each way. The going is very flat until you get to the Brough at NGR HY 596 087. Then the path is very steep down and a literal cliff hanger going up. I have three things to say here. Firstly this site is unmissable. Secondly, don't go if you have vertigo and thirdly, pick your weather. A very strong wind could make your visit dangerous.

On arrival at the top of the Brough, some 30m above the sea, you will first see the chapel. Excavations by Chris Morris in the 1980's showed that it was built in 2 phases: in the late 10th or early 11th century, a small chapel was built in wood; a short interval followed when it seems the chapel disappeared and then a stone chapel was built in the 12th century on the same spot. A very few burials were inserted. The next main work was the reconstruction of the ruin in the late 20th century.

Most of the rest of the buildings on the stack now consist of very low turf covered foundations. Apart from three they are original and unreconstructed. Immediately surrounding the chapel is a rectangular enclosure. This is in its turn surrounded by several small hut foundations. Outside, and to the north of that are many oval or bowed wall rectangular buildings. Two rows are built at right angles to a trackway which runs between them. At the south-east end of the track, and apparently on top of earlier buildings, is a stone built building investigated in recent excavations.

Water would have been available from the well that is situated in a large hollow near the place where the present day path joins the summit. It is a sump rather than a permanent spring.

The smaller hollows around this area are said to be shell holes. The Brough was used as target practice from ships at sea in both World Wars, and several pieces of shell casing have been retrieved here from time to time.

If the grass is long it may take you quite a time to make out all of this. So spring, before the summer growth, is the best time to visit. An enclosing wall runs along the cliff edge on the land side of the Brough.

It is clear that there is an as yet uninvestigated Pictish phase of occupation, into which later Scandinavian style structures were dug. The nature of this settlement has not been determined. But in the last few years excavations directed by James Barrett have made significant inroads into the mysteries of the Viking Age Brough. Based on area excavations over two houses he has found that the first Scandinavian people arrived in the 10th century, when a "street" of bowsided turf walled buildings was created along the North side of the Brough. At that time the entrance was at the South West corner of the Brough. Judging from the finds it seems that men, women and children all lived on this stacksite, year round. The houses here differ from others in more hospitable locations in Orkney in that they do not show any evidence of having cattle byres attached (for obvious reasons!). Presumably this is the settlement of a great chief and his household which would have been maintained through the production of his estates elsewhere in Orkney.

Whilst the site can be compared to the Brough of Birsay in many respects, there is a lack of evidence for a comparable 11th/12th century monastic settlement on this site in Deerness.

We can speculate that at times the Brough may have been the resort of an Earl of Orkney- or maybe Thorkell the Fosterer? According to Orkneyinga Saga he based himself on a stack in Caithness for some time when Orkney got too hot for him. Perhaps he had just such a residence closer to home?

At the highest point of the Brough a stone built longhouse was created. This building seems to have lasted like the others, with modifications, from the 10th to the 12th centuries. At a hundred feet above sea level it commands panoramic views of the sea approaches to eastern Orkney. The director of excavations, James Barrett, bottom right, is pictured with some of his team.

Hogback grave stone, Skaill, Deerness

This 11th-century grave stone was discovered in the kirkyard at Skaill. It would have been placed on a grave. It is a stone representation of a Norse house with a tiled roof. This particular stone has a relatively straight "roofline", but in many the stone represents the construction of a wooden aisled long-house with bowed sides and a curved apex to the roof – hence this style of grave marker being known as a hogback. The stone is currently housed in the annex to the church (inset), which was built in 1796, replacing the magnificent 12th-century church with two towers that once stood nearby.

    The word "Skaill" itself comes from the Old Norse word "Skali" which refers to the kind of feasting hall where in Viking times the great families of Orkney would entertain and do deals with their political enemies and friends, and maintain their warrior bands. For instance Swein Asleifarson from Gairsay (said to have been the last of the Vikings) kept 80 men at his hall through the winter time. After his death his son subdivided the building. It was a symbolic act of his joining the then modern world.

Skaill, Deerness

These came from the excavations of Skaill, Deerness that happened in the 1970's. All these and many hundreds more objects, including a multitude of pieces of pottery, could have been lost to us if the excavations had not taken place. This site is a key excavation for understanding of the development of Orcadian society from the Bronze Age into the Iron Age.

These objects and many more from the site are on display in the Orkney Museum at Tankerness House, Kirkwall.

Weaving Comb from Skaill. A common artefact found at Iron Age sites.

Bronze Age weapon from Skaill. A rare find.

Ingot mould, later Iron Age, from excavations at Skaill. These moulds are likely to have been used to accumulate the last drops from each casting, until enough bronze has been saved to heat again.

Jewellery mould, later Iron Age, to cast a ring shaped brooch. After the piece was turned out, the decorative detail would be added.

West Mainland

Breckness, Stromness

Breckness House HY 224 093 is reached by a walk (low tide), or a scramble (high tide), along the shore from the car park at Warbeth, on the outskirts of Stromness. Its main feature is the romantic ruin of a late medieval hall-house. Parts of the walls are unstable and you are advised not to approach too closely. The house may well have a more complicated history, but the present house was built in 1633 by George Graham, Bishop of Orkney. It is L-shaped, with entrances on the east side and south sides. From the east, the first room entered is the great kitchen – ahead is a stone stair up to the hall above. To the left of the door, entry could be had to grand rooms overlooking the sea. The house had many outbuildings and stables attached, parts of which are visible as turf covered archaeology. A small chapel and burial ground lay close to the cliff edge, where now some skeletons are eroding out. And this chapel was itself situated on a broch. From the shore you can see many walls of the Iron Age buildings, and a section through the broch ditch can be seen from the beach, west beyond the site. The discovery a few years ago of a stone with runic carvings on it, re-used in one of the 19th century farm buildings close by, implies that there is also a high status Norse site here.

Broch of Borwick, Sandwick

The broch of Borwick HY 224 167 is sliding gently into the sea off the top of some pretty impressive Atlantic facing cliffs. It is got to by a short walk from Yesnaby car park. Each broch is unique and has its own story to tell. This one is a rarity in that there are not many brochs on cliffs in Orkney – they are more usually in the heart of good land. The interior has been burnt, and that is also unusual. The doorway to this broch faces east and away from the sea – at Midhowe in Rousay sea-views to the south-west are framed by the door. Although brochs have many design and construction elements in common, their differences and particular histories have the potential to contribute individually to the understanding of Iron Age society as a whole. Questions as to whether or not the Broch of Borwick was burned as an act of aggression come into the long-running debate as to whether they are essentially military constructions.

When visiting this broch you need to be aware that once you are inside there is not a lot between you and a big drop into the sea!

The bone comb (see insert) from this broch is now on display in Orkney Museum, Kirkwall, it may have been used for weaving.

Rousay

Midhowe broch, Rousay

Previous page: Midhowe broch, Rousay. The stunning stone sea-defences below the broch have lasted half a century, through many a storm, in a very exposed location. They demonstrate what is possible.

Above: is one house of the broch village at Midhowe HY 371 305 on the Westness walk. It is easy to miss because it was built within the ditch. Each room that makes up the house would have been individually roofed, and most rooms had their own hearth. The house is very well appointed with small cupboards and a fancy little cantilevered stairway up onto the bank. Outside, one area was devoted to metalwork. This house was probably built sometime after 300 AD. At about the same time the interior of the broch was subdivided into two, and parts of it relined with neat stonework, that incorporates stones built on edge. This style of building replaces the coarser stonework and monumental archaeology that characterises the era of broch building. It seems that in the later Iron Age the Picts became more interested in the finer things of life, such as art and jewellery and spent their surpluses on that rather than making large architectural statements.

In a mile or so, the Westness Walk includes not only the broch, and a huge stalled chambered tomb that are in the care of the State; but also the remains of a medieval tower, a church, remains of crofts abandoned due to the 19th century clearances, an eroding and unrecorded broch, another chambered cairn, half of an Iron Age house, the remains of a 12th century long house, the site of a pagan Viking cemetery and a 12th century boat house.

Viera Lodge broch, Rousay

Left: a cist has been inserted into a cut in the natural rock HY 391 280. The close up (right, below) shows some Iron Age pottery that is falling out of it. This pot is pictured at about half its real size. You can see by the curve of the sherds that you are looking at the interior of the broken pot. The characteristic sandwich effect of orange outer and grey inner layers, shown in the broken edges, catch the eye and also help to distinguish it immediately from stone. The green slime comes later when the sea air gets to it.

Stone boxes or cists such as this have many reasons for being. For instance inserted in a bog, they are wells, lined with clay and inserted in a floor they can be water tanks. Under a cairn or mound they often contain ashes that are the remains of cremated people. Presumably this one was not created for the purpose of containing two or three broken pots –its original purpose might become clear in context. Luckily most of this broch is still safe. In a tiny exposure like this, we are not going to find out much more about it.

Gateway to the Atlantic Project at Swandro

A series of coastally eroding sites along the Westness shore provides an international team from several universities an opportunity to look in detail at changes through time. The short growing season here at 59° north means subsistence economies can be balanced on a knife edge. We are ideally located therefore to look at how people, through thousands of years of cultural change and varying climatic conditions, have adapted to living here. This part of the project is looking at a site that spans several hundreds of years. The oldest deposits are exposed at the bottom of the beach, below the low tide mark. The later ones - those relating to an Iron age building, perhaps another broch - are coming out at higher levels. This project is making the best of these sites that cannot be saved from the sea.

Next page: Maltbarn Pier, Eday.

Eday

Calf of Eday, Salt Works

These salt works were built on the shores of the Calf of Eday, at NGR HY 574 391 and 575 384, probably some time in the 17th century, by the laird of Eday, whose mansion house sits across the Sound. He would have been able to take a stroll in his gardens and note the peat smoke and activity at his factory across the water. To get here you need to hire a boat to the Calf.

Carrick House, Eday gets a special mention here because it has great sea-connections being the location of the notorious Pirate Gow's capture and imprisonment. His boat ran aground on the Calf, and he was subsequently lured by the tricksy laird of Carrick, and a lot of drink, into captivity. And if you visit in the summer time when the house is open, you can decide for yourself if the Pirate's blood stains on the floor in Carrick House are archaeology, or legend.

Calf of Eday, chambered cairns

The salt works were put up to make salt through boiling seawater over fires that burnt peat. The remains of long peat stacks lie up behind the ruinous buildings. An encounter with industrial archaeology on an uninhabited island! Whereas the exact arrangements for boiling the sea water here are unknown, elsewhere it seems that sea water was taken up in buckets, boiled in long shallow iron tanks, the water skimmed to clean it of visible impurities and the salt scooped then into long thin willow or straw baskets which were hung up to dry. A very labour intensive operation. But very much more worthwhile when salt taxes were high and avoidable!

On the way to the salt works look out for the two Neolithic chambered cairns. The two-storey chambered cairn faces directly back across the sound to Eday. The interior of the lower chamber can be seen bottom right. If you walk around up to the top of the cairn you are right next to a prehistoric quarry. The larger cairn (above right) is further up the hill and is topped by a wall that may have been built in the Iron Age: following it a little way will lead you to a partially excavated Iron Age house.

Maltbarn Eday

Maltbarn at HY 564 288 is very close to the pier pictured on page 35. The shore section contains several periods of occupation from recent centuries and back into prehistory. 25 years ago the eroding section was seen as representing the remains of a high status Norse dwelling. Recent excavations have identified some medieval and post medieval buildings, but nothing that would necessarily be interpreted in that way. Amanda Brend of ORCA directed the excavation that undertook the tricky job of unpicking this erosion face. She has provided the drawing below, with the various phases identified.

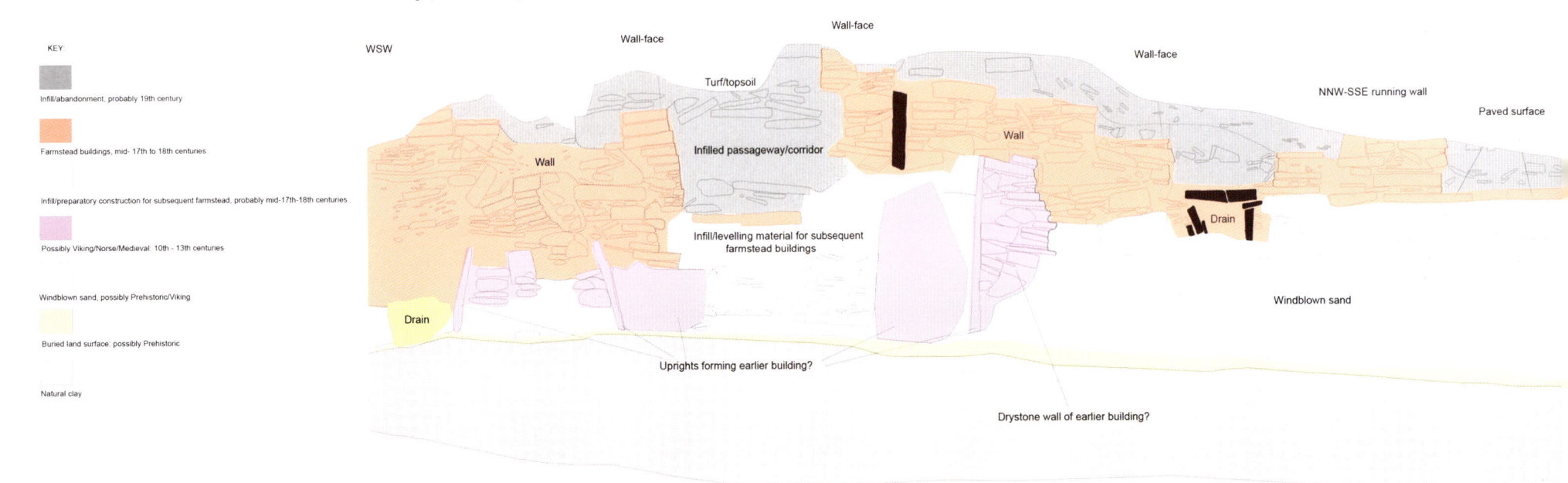

KEY:
- Infill/abandonment, probably 19th century
- Farmstead buildings, mid-17th to 18th centuries
- Infill/preparatory construction for subsequent farmstead, probably mid-17th-18th centuries
- Possibly Viking/Norse/Medieval: 10th – 13th centuries
- Windblown sand, possibly Prehistoric/Viking
- Buried land surface: possibly Prehistoric
- Natural clay

Stronsay

The Danes Pier Stronsay

There is some discussion as to whether or not this is an entirely natural feature, which it could be. But there are elements that look built. Best viewed at low tide, it extends quite a way out. The broch close by has been partially dug out, leaving some chambers within the walls viewable from above. If you lie down you can look in safely. And between the broch and the Danes Pier, you will see the remains of banks and ditches running across the neck of land cutting off the broch and headland. HY 690 214.

Lamb Head broch, Stronsay

Tams Castle, Stronsay

This is the bigger of two natural rock stacks in Odin Bay at NGR HY 689 234. It supports a building that may well have been a hermitage site built by monks. It is not known how old it is, but it could either have been built in the Norse period or it could be the work of Early Christian monks of the Pictish or Celtic churches. The name suggests a dedication to St Thomas. Until one or two of these sites on stacks have been at least partly excavated, they could be more or less anything!!

Ward of Housebay, Stronsay

The nature of this site is not known. But a site's position in the landscape is important. The name Ward of Houseby indicates that it may have been used as a beacon site during the Viking or medieval period. Due to its size and prominent position, it is suggested the site represented by the large mound may have been a Neolithic chambered cairn, or perhaps a broch. Some fragments of Iron Age pottery have been found here. The same, and as it turns out, very wrong, suggestions were made for the Knowe of Skea (Westray) prior to its investigation (see below).

Westray

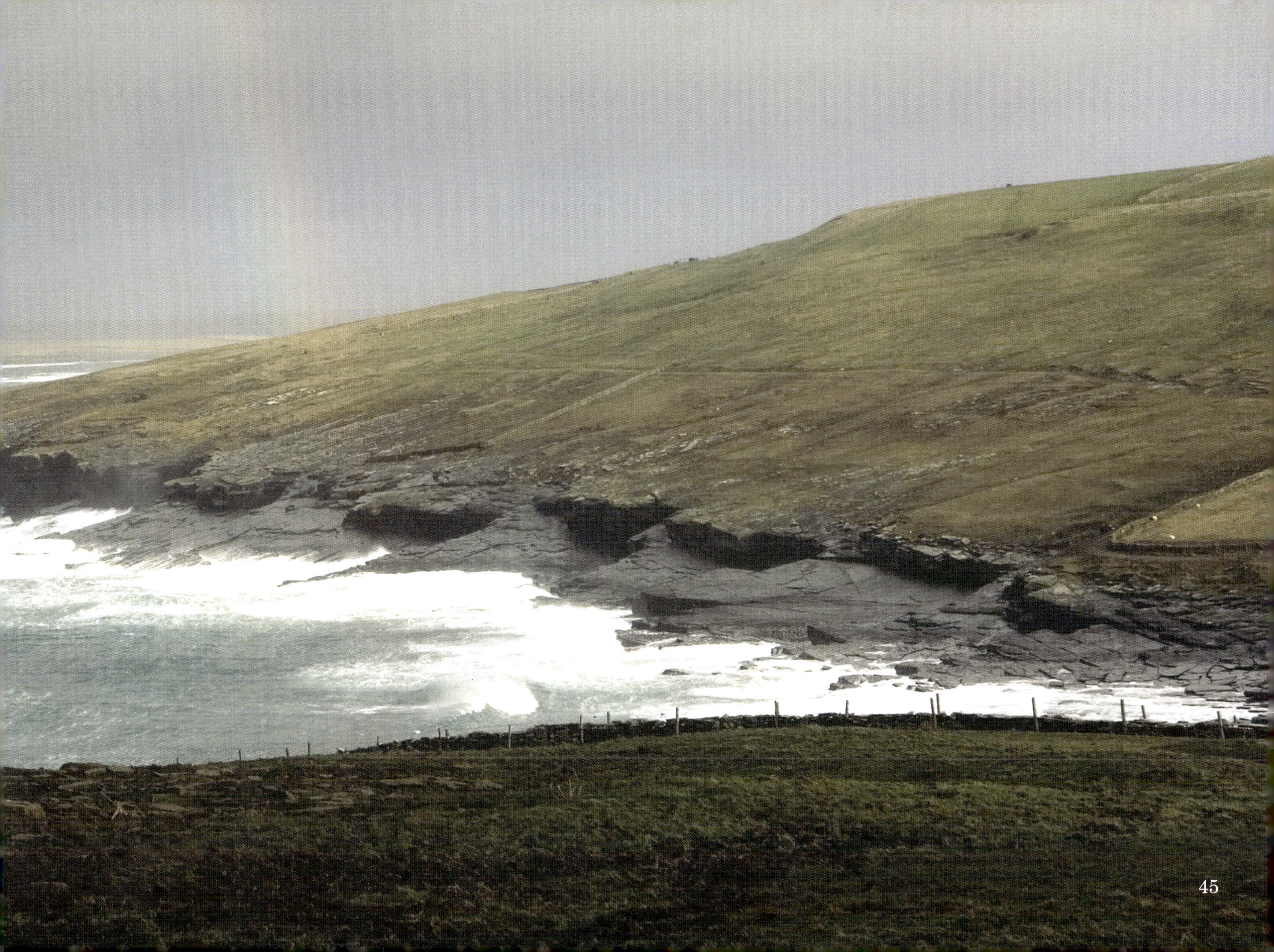

The Mortuary House, Knowe of Skea

One of the peculiar and unique features of this Iron Age building uncovered on the Ness. This "doorway" is tiny and the stair passage behind leads only into the thickness of the walls. How can this be explained?

Knowe of Skea, Berstness, Westray

The Knowe of Skea HY 441 418 site is one of the most exciting discoveries to be made in Scotland in a decade. Its strange nature was identified through excavation. It consists of an Iron Age mortuary house, cemetery and other buildings, many associated with metalworking. The site was occupied for some hundreds of years into the Pictish era. The photos were taken at an early stage in the excavation.

This site was included in a programme of test trenching eroding sites to determine their nature and importance. All that was known at the start of excavation was that this mound, at the extreme end of a peninsula and now sometimes cut off by the tide, had Iron Age pottery coming out from its erosion faces. It had been thought to be a broch. The team of excavators led by Graeme Wilson and Hazel Moore started by putting in small test trenches, which demonstrated the monumentality of the site and something of its nature, but it defied interpretation for some time. Nothing of this sort had been found before. One theory after another was proposed, tested and rejected. Inside the mortuary house fixtures and fittings made it appear as a house might, but only a very few rather beautiful personal objects were found, and these were placed in "beds" in the building. There was a distinct lack of normal domestic activity represented. The walls were unusually massive. The "passage" (seen in the previous photo) leading in from the outside goes nowhere. There is a real entrance at the other end of the building.

Around this house are several others. Metalworking was undertaken in many of the buildings. The photo on page (page 49) shows the excavations just as the exterior buildings were beginning to be examined. And everywhere there were burials. People were buried in rubble all around the main building. Some were formally placed in cists. Some had been wrapped in shrouds that were fastened by pins made on site. Some were so tightly packed in their graves it is thought they may have been allowed to partly decompose, and then they were tightly bound with their knees right up against the chest. Many skeletons of babies were found on this site, raising the possibility that the people practised infanticide. It looks like all members of the community could have been buried in this place.

Over a hundred skeletons have been found at this site. This will provide opportunities to study the people, their family relationships, their diseases, and their beliefs. The remains of this community provide a unique opportunity for Scotland, where burials of this period are extremely rare.

Many of the bodies seem just to have been roughly placed within the rubble of the buildings and the excavators think that the burials may well have been the final act of a lengthy suite of ceremonies or rites associated with people's death. And that perhaps for the Iron Age people using this cemetery the processes between death and burial (perhaps undertaken in the mortuary house) were more important to the well-being of the souls of the departed, and of the living who were burying them, than the final disposal of the remains. (Graeme Wilson pers. comm).

This site will increase our knowledge of the Iron Age Scottish population by leaps and bounds – the burials here form about 90 per cent of all those known in Scotland as a whole. And of course in Orkney, where DNA studies are often carried out in pursuit of the "Blood of the Vikings" we should now have potential for data that will enable us to understand whether there was a sea-change in the racial origins of the population following the Norse take-over, or whether the indigenous population continued to live here, changing gradually with the times.

Knowe of Skea, Berstness, Westray

The buildings shown here were founded upon, and surrounded by human remains. Some buildings were used for metal working. After their reduction to rubble, more interments took place. The whole site was abandoned in the later Iron Age. It was to be re-used as a fish-drying platform at some point in the medieval period.

Links of Noltland, Westray

The "petals" of this stone flower are the collapsed remains of a kelp pit. The archaeology of this 18th- and 19th-century "boom and bust" industry is everywhere. Kelping involved cutting, heaping, drying, and burning seaweed. These pits are where the seaweed was burnt. A glassy slag would be scooped out of the pit and sold on to the chemical and glass industry. According to Willie Thomson (Kelp-Making in Orkney, 1983) 3,000 Orcadians made at least part of their living from kelp when the trade was at its peak. And many of the Orkney lairds became extremely rich on the proceeds. By the late 1830's the industry had virtually disappeared - although some production trickled on for another hundred years.

   This photo also illustrates a difficulty of understanding the archaeology of sand: the kelp pit itself will have been dug into the turf when ground level was higher. The stones around the edge would just have cleared the level of the turf. Now the sandy soils round and about it, and beneath it, have gradually dried and blown away, leaving this relatively recent feature to settle on prehistoric soils.

In 2007 it was thought little remained of this building...

...by 2012 it is clear that this same Bronze Age house retains deep, undisturbed, deposits.

Links of Noltland, Westray

The Links of Noltland contain a rich landscape from the late Neolithic and Early Bronze age. Houses, fields and funerary monuments of the era were buried by blown sand and this has conserved them very well for 4 or 5 thousand years. But in last 30 years the protective grass topped sand dunes were very badly burrowed by rabbits and then the sand blew away. This revealed the first Neolithic houses, partially excavated in the 1970's and taken into the care of the Government. Attempts were made then to retain cover by planting marram grass but to no avail. A low tech solution of sand bagging a small area was more successful, lasting over twenty years. Historic Scotland has now embarked on a major campaign to excavate everything as quickly as possible since the remains are deemed to be unsustainable. They are also trying a substantial landscaping solution, attempting to conserve the site by taking sand from the top of the dunes, where there is no known archaeology and re-depositing it on the shore edge to form a bund.

Westray Wife, Links of Noltland

The skull pictured above is one of many cow skulls placed horn to horn in a ring beneath the encircling wall of a Neolithic house in the Links of Noltland. A comparable deposit, of an encircling pile of cattle leg bones around a building at the Ness of Brodgar, serves to demonstrate the significant place of cattle in Neolithic society.

Dubbed "The Westray Wife", this tiny sandstone lady is only 41mm high. She is thought to be Neolithic and the earliest representation of a person yet to be found in Scotland. She was excavated from a midden deposit in the Neolithic village in the Links.

Cross Kirk, Tuquoy, Westray

This 12th-century church has been considerably altered and extended since the days when it was put up – possibly by Haflidi Thorkelsson, the son of one of Orkney's "leading families" in Westray. He was "unpopular" and his father said to be "very able but overbearing"(Orkneyinga Saga chapter 56). The grand farm now eroding from the shore near to the Cross Kirk is likely to have been theirs. In the 19th century the church was much robbed for stone, but it is recorded that at the time an old inhabitant had begged the people taking down the walls not to "pull down the Danes' work". His words saved the building and now the ruin is in State care in a well kept burial ground. NGR HY 455 431.

Tuquoy, Westray

On the shore below and immediately to the west of the Kirk, a different story of is told. The archaeological remains of a grand house or castle and many other buildings, drains, middens, walls are being eroded by the sea, over a length of some 120 metres. The site extends inland for some 50 metres. This site has had a small excavation focussed on part of the erosion face. Amongst the many great finds at this site was a rune stone that read "Thorstein Einarsson carved these runes", and a pit full of well preserved waterlogged wood indicating the import of dressed timber from Scandinavia that was then further worked at the farm.

The black plastic that is emerging from the erosion face marks the line between excavated and backfilled site (above) and unexcavated archaeology below. Due to the evident importance of the site an attempt to reduce the erosion at this site was made. Box gabions (wire crates) filled with stones were placed in front of the section. These lasted some years, but are now destroyed.

Castle of Burrian, Westray

Better known for its puffins, this stack site was created naturally by erosion of the surrounding cliffs. On the top of the stack are two bow-sided buildings, between 9 and 10 metres long; one with a circular structure at its west end. It is thought to have been used as a hermitage by early Christian or medieval monks. Several stack sites are known from around Orkney. The ideas of spiritual discipline developed through isolation and hardship, with any tendencies to pride being tempered by reliance on God and on being tended by the community, were occasionally fashionable throughout the centuries. None of these sites have yet been excavated in Orkney, so it is not yet known who lived here, or when. On a wild day of wind it would be difficult to imagine that it was possible at all. Perhaps like some of the lighthouse keepers of the recent past, the monks would have tethered themselves to prevent being blown away. NGR HY 503 429. And see Tams Castle, Stronsay.

Evertaft, Westray

This site on the north-east coast at NGR HY 455 512 is a settlement mound now more than half gone as judged by its profile, which peaks at the erosion face. Yet it is still somewhat more than 3m in height. It is likely to have been inhabited since the later Iron Age. There are clean sand layers within the mound indicating times when it may have been abandoned.

At the top of this mound you used to be able to see the remains of fragments of coal and slate in the sand. Coal was a reverse cargo for kelp and slate, once exported from Westray and indicates that the site may have been used to load and off-load bulk cargoes in the 18th and 19th centuries. This patch has now gone for good, and you can see very little that could be related to this activity or date. The uppermost exposed layers look at a guess to be 16th or 17th century. Beneath all that blocky stone work you see layer upon layer of settlement and midden. In the photos taken the day we visited in 2006, a major collapse obscured many of the lower layers. The detail is of an area seen to the upper right of the section. It focuses on a wall that is coming straight towards the camera. A large stone is slumping out bottom right of that wall, as it is undermined. There does not seem to be any clay bonding to this wall, which you might expect of a later medieval or early modern house wall. In the absence of associated finds, we are left speculating as to what this may represent, or how old it may be.

Hodgalee, Broch, Westray

Situated at the north eastern side of the Bay of Tuquoy, at NGR HY 464 447, a walk along the beach at low tide is all it takes to get to one of the fastest eroding sites in Orkney. The losses here are an archaeological disaster. The site consists of what is probably a broch on the headland and another sort of Iron Age site hard by to the east. It is the latter which is rapidly disappearing. This site is, up to now, as well preserved as Skara Brae was. Dwellings likely to be about 2000 years old, and with exceptional potential for artefactual and ecofactual preservation and with 3D architecture still intact, are disappearing.

This is the view you get when coming round the shore to Hodgalee. The great broch mound that seems more or less complete is topped out by two enormous nousts that were used into the 20th century. A noust is a place for putting a boat ashore – they consist of low stone or turf walls that stand only to a few feet in height – sufficient to save the wind getting in too much under the boat. Winter nousts are higher up the banks, further away from the sea, where boats would be beached for extended periods; whereas, summer nousts are closer to the sea for "overnight parking". It is more or less impossible to tell how old a noust might be, just by looking at it. Nousts like these resemble the shape of Viking long boats, and yet when a similar one was excavated, dating evidence of an old Bovril jar (c. 1950!) was discovered. By contrast at Westness, in Rousay, a Norse boat house (dated to the 11th or 12th centuries) was rectangular and had a cobbled ramp at the rear to provide grip for a horse or cow to help tow the boat ashore.

2007

2012

Hodgalee, Iron-age buildings, Westray

Next to the broch a 50m stretch of Iron Age archaeology is being trashed. A few years ago an outer wall of a round house and a nearby doorway could be seen in the shore section, looking directly out to sea. The stone lintel on the top of the door was about knee high. The walls of the houses themselves disappeared beneath the storm beach. Only 40 years ago, Westray children ventured inside these rooms. Now, we have lost those walls and doorways and the sea is inside the houses themselves. Geophysics shows that there is still a substantial amount to the rear of what is visible at present, and material probably remains in situ under the beach.

Hodgalee, Westray

Here the single-skin construction of some of the walls can be seen in profile. The wall at the rear is the same one curving around forming part of a chamber. This site is obviously very vulnerable to the next large gale or high tide.

Right: a fulmar's nest has been made from the dump of cockle shells in an Iron Age midden.

Hodgalee, Westray

This fulmar is in defence mode. You need to give them a wide berth to avoid being spewed on. And beware of their very charming and fluffy babies who have equal ability over the distance and, allegedly, greater accuracy than their parents. If you, or your dog are sicked on it is very difficult to get rid of the stinking fishy oil. Fulmars love archaeology: they like to have a roof over their heads, and often nest in eroding drains or other similar structures.

Quoygrew Westray

Excavations by James Barrett discovered a settlement mound that spanned 1000 years, from the 10th century. A single long house, repaired, reworked and extended, lasted over 700 years. James was prompted to undertake his work by the rich midden that could be seen eroding on the shore. It was full of the large cod bones that are seen here in these islands as a sign of a Norse site of c.1000AD. After 400 years of solidly Scandinavian type material culture, including e.g. a preference for imported soapstone, suddenly in the 15th century Scottish pottery began to appear in the rooms. Here in this very ordinary house we can see reflected in its material culture the lasting political trend of the Scottification of Orkney.

After six summer seasons of work, the community created a project to consolidate and protect the building. As with all hard engineered sea walls, the power of the sea is deflected and probably increases the erosion at the ends. Although there is clearly midden and structures beyond and under the storm beach, the wall is doing its job of protecting a long stretch of shore, and providing and protecting an interpreted, sustainable, monument.

The story of the Orcadian fish trade from the 11th century can be made out through study of the fish bones themselves. Butchery marks show cod being processed and dried as "stock fish" for the market. It is likely that oil would have been extracted from fish livers (as evidenced at St Boniface, Papa Westray).

Trenabie and Quoygrew, Westray

Here, only 100m from the site at Quoygrew is another exposure, looking suspiciously like the one that first attracted James Barrett to excavate. Stone walls and floor surfaces can be made out. Large fish bones can be seen in the midden, thus this site too is likely to be 10th to 13th century, and contemporary with Quoygrew. This area of Trenabie is clearly the focus of an extensive settlement easily comparable to Shetland's iconic "Jarlshof" in size.

Knowe of Burristae, Westray

The shoreside location of so many of Orkney's brochs means that they are an endangered species. This one at NGR HY 431 429 was built into a boggy area and the ground behind it remains wet to this day. It is quite common for brochs to be built into wetland or lochs, with access via a narrow causeway or stepping stones. Many are built within enclosing ditches or banks. Whether this type of setting was chosen or created for defensive purposes or whether the design and construction of brochs was made to incorporate in stone a mass of symbolism related to earthly and spiritual power is a hot topic of debate.

The sea has taken about half of the broch, and is eroding it at floor level. On the gently sloping shore upright stones, hearth remains, and other floor level features cut into the natural clay can be seen. A thin layer of very dark brown peaty material is visible beneath the stones on the beach. It seems this is natural and earlier than the broch. This is an interesting feature, for bogs offer an opportunity for preservation of materials normally destroyed during the course of time: wood and leather for instance.

Burristae, Westray

The exposed stonework here is at first floor level. Despite being excavated by antiquarians, and half lost to the sea there is still an amazing amount remaining in these buildings.

Pierowall Westray

"On Sunday Earl Rognvald had mass celebrated in the village. As they were standing outside the church, they saw sixteen men approaching unarmed and with their hair close cut. The Earl's men thought their dress singular, and spoke amongst themselves of who they might be. Then the Earl made a ditty:

> *Sixteen have I seen together,*
> *With a small tuft on their foreheads;*
> *Surely these are women coming,*
> *All without their golden trinkets.*
> *Now may we of this bear witness*
> *In the west here all the maidens*
> *Wear their hair short…"*

The Earl in the quote from Joseph Anderson's translation of Orkneyinga Saga was the poet, world traveller, crusader, bon-viveur, and finally saint, Earl Rognvald Kali Kolsson, who ruled Orkney in the first half of the 12th century. He was clearly making jokes about a group of monks. If the Saga is correct, which some doubt, he was likely to be standing at the door of St Mary's in Pierowall, which was then a large enough settlement to be called a village. The importance of this part of Westray to Orkney and the western Viking world is reinforced by the several pagan Viking graves that were placed in the dunes behind the settlement. It has been suggested that Pierowall could have been the site of a beach market in the 9th and 10th centuries, as this arrangement of burials behind a village on a beach is a pattern seen in Scandinavia, at famous market sites such as Birka in Sweden.

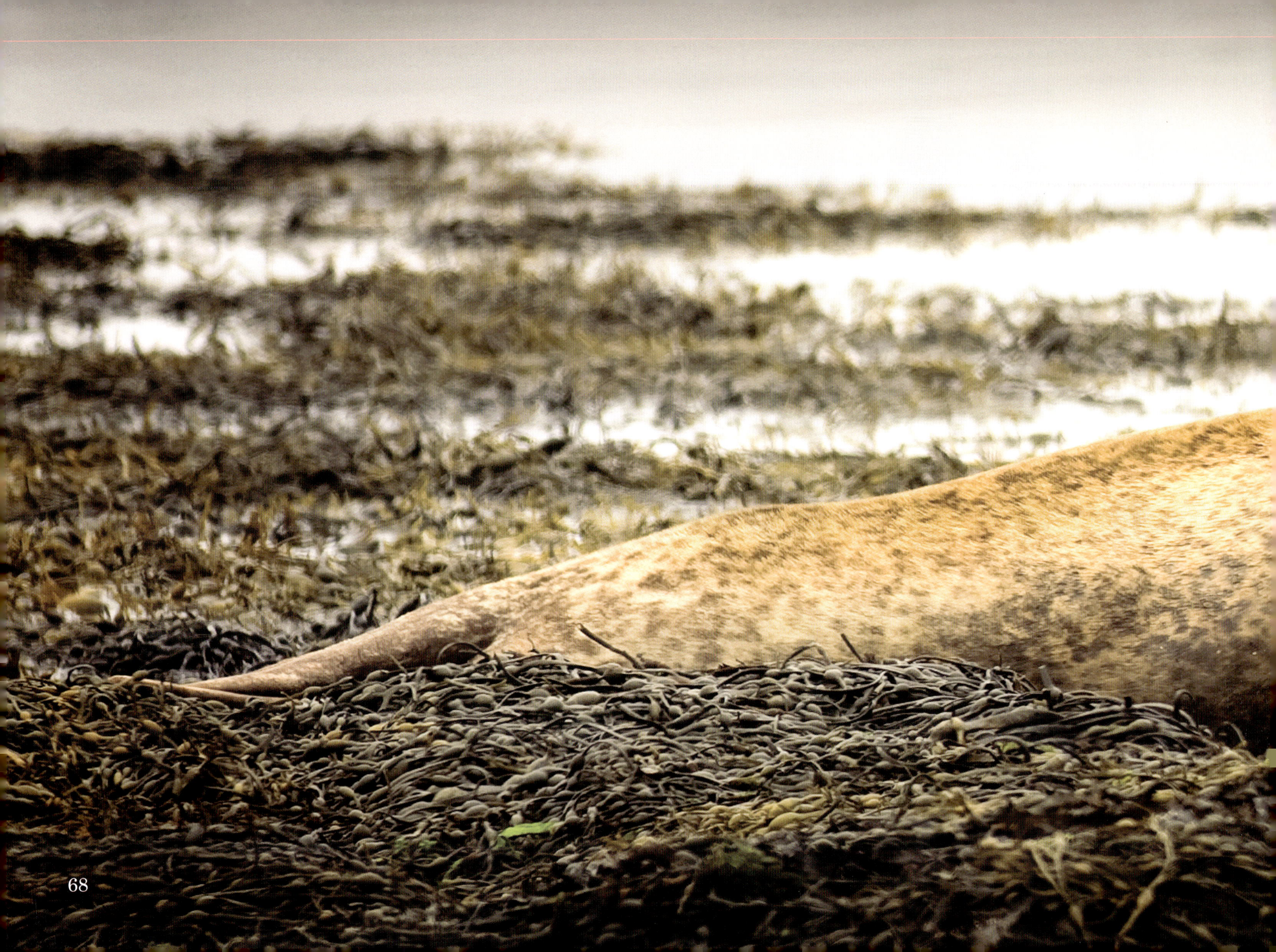

Papa Westray

St Boniface and Munkerhoose, Papa Westray

This charming little stone is about 5 foot long, much smaller than Skaill's hogback. It is still in the churchyard of the chapel which is built on the medieval foundations of the chapel dedicated to St Boniface. The chapel (well worth a visit in its own right) is set back from the shore, but is inextricably associated with the settlement mound that is exposed by coastal erosion a hundred metres away. A carved stone (now on display in Orkney Museum) was found on the shore nearby several years ago, at the exposure known as Munkerhoose, and has been interpreted as part of an 8th century shrine. It has been suggested that this island could have been the centre of an Orcadian bishopric in the 8th or 9th centuries AD. Whether or not that is correct, the upper layers of this mound probably are the remains of a substantial Norse monastery.

Munkerhoose and St Boniface, Papa Westray

The whole site of Munkerhoose and St Boniface covers two hectares and for much of that the archaeology is up to 4m deep. This weed-infested and eroding section represents archaeology from the Bronze Age through to the present. The shore deposits include a sequence which is part of the large ecclesiastical site, centred roughly at NGR HY488 526.

The director, Chris Lowe applied an excavation technique known as "Tapestry". The remains of his team's work can still be seen, in a series of "quarry faces" in which some elements of the site can be studied in plan, but in which it is mostly understood through the vertical section. The more usual method of excavation is simply to open wide areas in plan and then dig down stratigraphically, but this method on a deep site is very costly. The resultant excavation report (Lowe CE, 1998) shows Tapestry to have succeeded amazingly well on this site.

Munkerhoose and St Boniface, Papa Westray

Cows are pictured here strolling along the eroding face of the site. The ones with their backs to camera are where the "causeway" crosses an encircling ditch that was built to enclose the roundhouse and other dwellings in the middle Iron Age.

The upper layers of the soils that are rich in fish-bone and ash that were tipped here in the 12th century represent specialised and intensive fish processing on site. Perhaps the making of fish oil for lamps? Although creating a deep deposit, this activity was quite short lived, and its beginning and end may mark changes in political and/or religious power structures at the time.
In the fore and middle grounds the curving walls of the round house can be seen emerging from the section.

Knap of Howar, Papa Westray

Here in the middle of the west side of Papay is the oldest upstanding house in northwest Europe. It was built nearly 6,000 years ago. Yet today you can still crawl in through the front entrance, and shuffle through its linking passageway. The only missing parts are the roof and soft furnishings. You can see room divisions, parts of stone furniture, hearths and cupboards. Skara Brae is more famous, but this is older. These houses were first excavated in the 1930's. And in the 1970's Anna Ritchie and her team obtained the date of 3,800 BC from the middens. This is a site in the care of the State, and it has a fine sea-wall to keep erosion at bay. There are minor amounts of erosion here and there, and where rabbits burrow into middens oyster shells come to the surface. These are the debris of Neolithic meals, and perhaps reflect the slightly warmer temperatures of those times. Access to this site is free of charge and unrestricted. Out of season you are unlikely to meet anyone else here. NGR HY 483 518.

Knap of Howar, Papa Westray

These earlier Neolithic houses are laid out in a different way to the buildings that we are so familiar with at Skara Brae. Here the spaces within the buildings are separated by upright slabs and one passes through one space to get to another, which contrasts with many of the houses of later villages such as Skara Brae, Rinyo in Rousay, or Barnhouse at the Stones of Stenness, where a squared interior layout centred round the hearth prevails.

Weelies Taing, Papa Westray

This site is located on the north-east side of Papay at NGR HY 505 533. At first sight this seems so big that it is impossible that it could be anything other than natural, but a closer look makes it clear that a natural lagoon has been transformed. Here cobbling has made a road on top of the south side of the enclosure, and beyond many upright stones in various formations are inserted. Fish ponds and/or fish traps are quite usual features of medieval monasteries elsewhere, but in Orkney we have not definitely identified either. Still, it seems likely that this feature represents the remains of a medieval fish pond and traps. Excavations at Munkerhoose make it clear that fish-processing on an major scale was undertaken in the Middle Ages at the settlement mound related to St. Boniface church – perhaps it was the economic mainstay of the monastery? Today seals lie up on the rocks here in large numbers; they slip into the pond if you disturb them. There are so many that the smell of seal is strong here. You should not attempt to stroke baby seals, it frightens them and they will bite you. Apparently their teeth are really full of infection.

Weelies Taing, Papa Westray
Cobbles laid to enable a horse to help drag a net across the pond?

Fish trap.

Weelies Taing, Papa Westray
Fish trap.

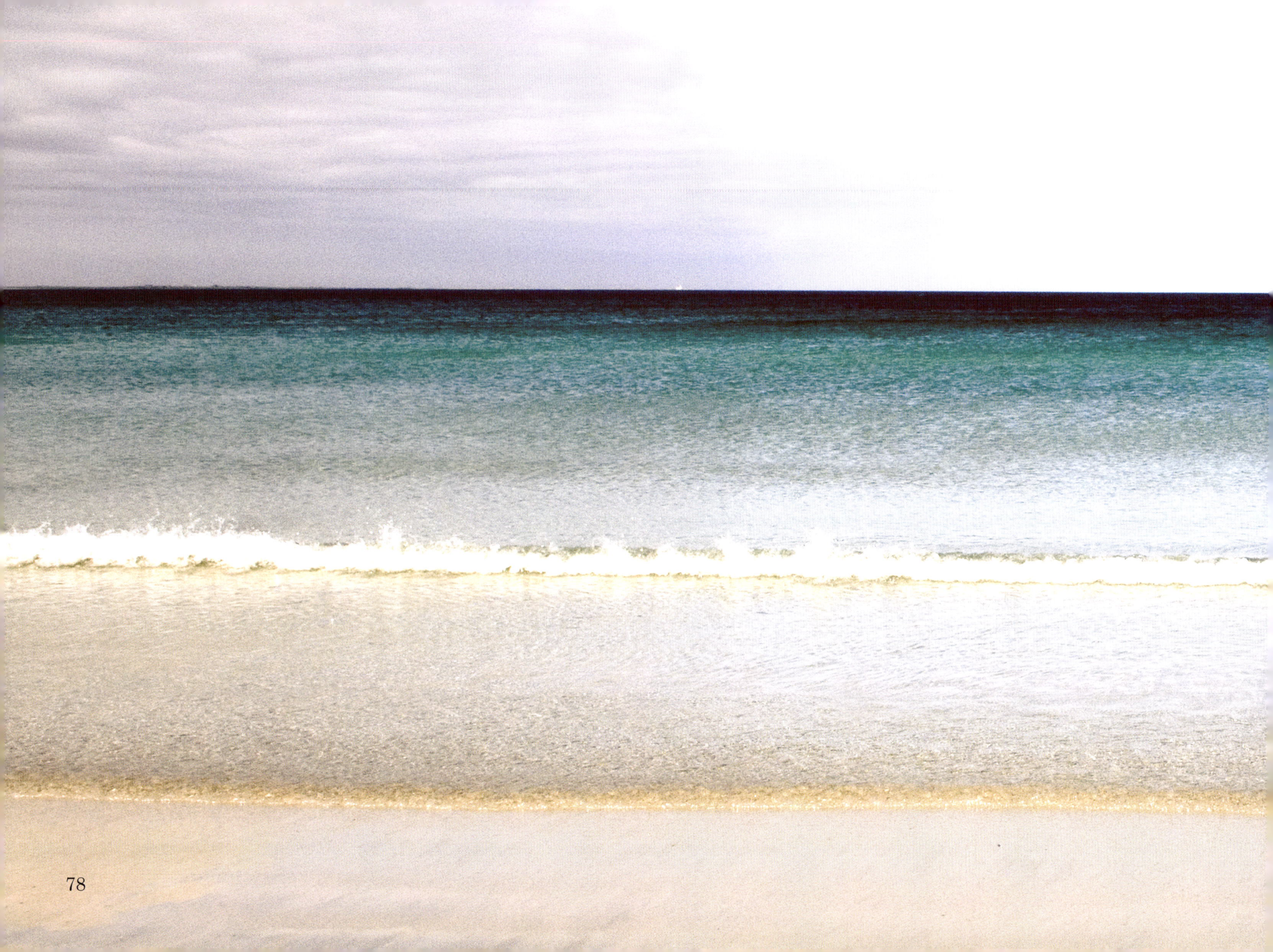

Sanday

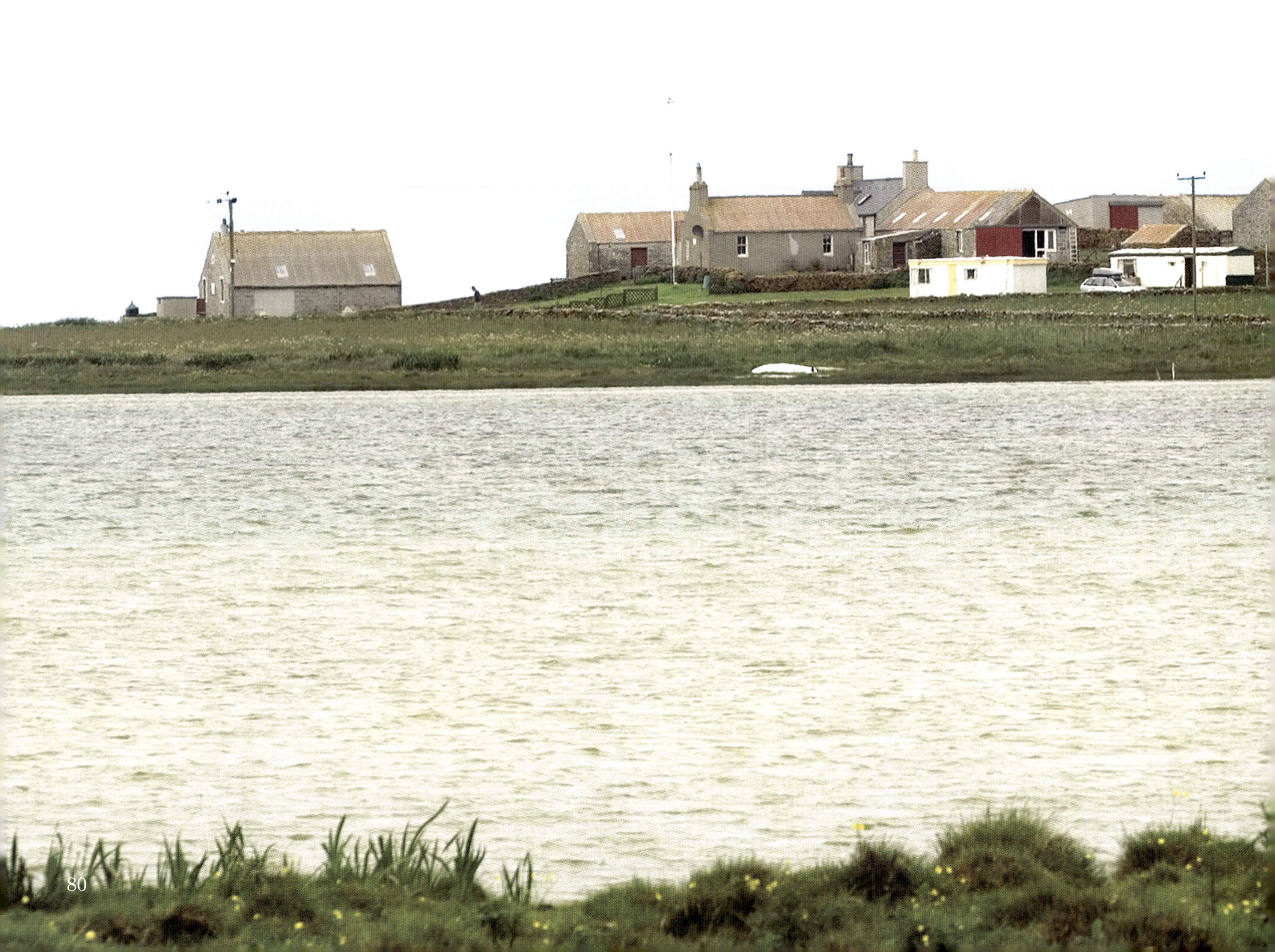

Tofts, Sanday

This is Tofts at the north end of Sanday. The whole hill on which the farm is situated has been created by people living on the spot for millennia. Much of Sanday is made up of these "farm mounds". The interiors of two of them as exposed by erosion can be seen later on in this section. In Orkney it is often the case that settlement has focussed for the last two or three thousand years in a discrete area (such as Skaill, Deerness, or Breckness) and that those settlements do create mounds within the landscape. But it is really only in Sanday, North Ronaldsay and Papa Westray where these huge mounds covering hectares developed to their fullest extent.

Newark, Sanday

The exposed erosion face of this classic farm mound is nearly 100 metres long. The visible stonework on the left-hand side emerges from the mound at about head height. It includes an under-floor box drain that probably dates from the 12th to 15th centuries AD. The mound may have taken some fifteen hundred years to accumulate — but there is no way to be certain until some work is done on the site, or diagnostic material is located by chance, in situ.

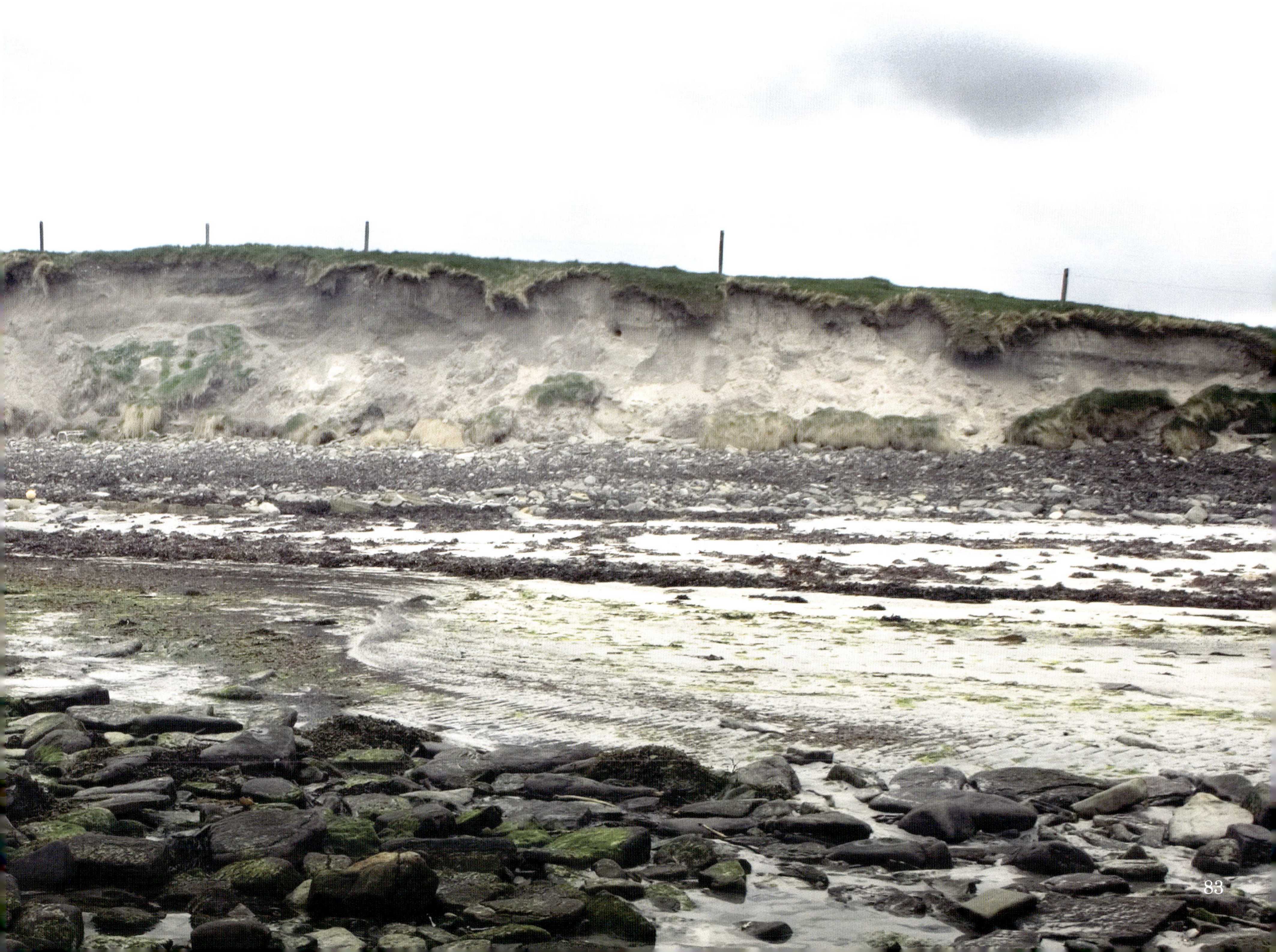

Fish Trap at Newark, Sanday

It is always problematic when looking at features that are now intertidal, to understand whether they were created to be so, or whether erosion has done the job. This rough circle has been part-built using the technique known as cassying. As this is a common method of building in stone on the shore because it withstands wave action very well, I think it is clear that we are dealing here with something that was intended to be in the sea. It may well be part of a fish trap, or pond.

Stove Farm, Sanday

The name "Stove" comes from Old Norse Stofa – a dwelling with a separate fire-house or living area. It is sometimes the case that Stove names recall the sites of impressive wooden Norwegian kit houses, imported in the medieval period by wealthy land owners. This site features in folk stories and was the site of the Episcopal chapel. Although the latter was 18th-century it is quite likely to have been built on the site of an earlier one. Stove is probably therefore a site of some antiquity, and high status. But the most extraordinary thing about Stove is the huge "model" farm. Built in the 19th century and boasting an enormous byre, it had a steam driven mill. The chimney is visible in the photo above. Milling was most important for preparing animal feed. The scale of this undertaking is overwhelming! NGR HY 611 355.

Stove Bay Neolithic Site, Sanday

The Stove Neolithic site is vast. From the shore at HY 612 353 it extends well back into the cultivated fields behind, where test-pitting produced many flints. Starting at the inland end of the exposed section, you will instantly notice the reddish gleam of peat-ashy soils, then a few house-walls in cross-section, with soils piled up against them. This continues for about 40 metres. A little further along the exposure you will come across a prehistoric cairn, of unknown date. Its central part is made of two long prone flagstones propped against each other. The cross section of this looks like an inverted V. Around this is a stony cairn. When it first came to view the tented stone structure was reported as containing ashes, but by the time I got to it, they had gone. I think this site may well once have contained both inhumation and cremation – since the V stones look like they were made to enclose a body.

Burnt Mound, Meur, Sanday

The burnt stone in this photo is the waste product resulting from stones being roasted in a fire and then cracking when put in water to heat it. This site, consisting of a complex of both upstanding and sunken tanks and drains and water inlets was revealed when the storm beach was temporarily taken away by the sea. Masses of fine yellow clay were used in water-proofing the large cist-like lidded tank, and on the floor of the structure. It was also paved in places. It is in a typical wet-land situation – take a peek across the road.

Excavations here were led by Ronan Toolis from AOC Scotland, with help from Sanday residents. The structures disappear back into the shore banks where they are either cut up or concealed by the road. Some remnants of the tanks may still be visible, depending on whether or not the storm beach is piled high, or dragged off into the sea. HY 746 457.

Tresness chambered cairn, Sanday

Sanday has the privilege of having at least three Neolithic chambered cairns eroding into the sea at present. The tranquil green mound in this photo belies the truth that this is one of the most spectacular of archaeological disasters I can think of. And Sanday specialises in spectacular archaeological disasters! On the page over, the exposed passage into the central chamber is pictured. There is at this site a complete section across the cairn – the passage in the photo is surrounded by masses of cairn material on each side (not illustrated). Lines of concentric walling surround the chamber, and stones are used to fill in between those single skins of walls. Thus a huge monument was created around a quite small chamber. The chamber at this site may never have been disturbed. But now the sea is licking into the passage. NGR HY 711 375.

Tresness chambered cairn, Sanday

Note the broken roof slabs and the entrance passage. In a lot of tombs it is reported that the passages are blocked externally and/or infilled from the top when the tomb finally goes out of use in the Neolithic. This may have happened here, but the exterior of the monument has gone into sea. It is not known if there are any human remains at risk in this monument, but of course it is likely.

Northskaill farm mound, Sanday

The puzzled young man (James Moore, Orkney College archaeologist) photographed here is over 6 foot tall. This eroding farm mound is notable for its lack of stony structures. It is mostly formed of ashy dumps and sandy soils. A while ago a composite bone comb of the 13th century AD was found eroding out of this mound at about the height of James' shoulder. NGR HY 683 444.

Bay of Lopness, Sanday

These stubby iron fragments are last remnants of the B98, a captured German destroyer that was driven ashore in 1919. Here the boilers and turbines are exposed at low tide. NGR HY 746 441

North Ronaldsay

Broch of Burrian, North Ronaldsay

This site at NGR HY 762 513 was excavated in the 1870's by W. Traill, the North Ronaldsay proprietor, whose antiquarian interests and techniques were very advanced for the era. He distinguished phases of occupation at this site, through the use of stratigraphy.

The shallow coastline and soft soils here provide no protection against the sea. Each year more is lost from this site.

North Ronaldsay

Broch of Burrian finds, North Ronaldsay

The 19th century excavation of this monument produced many fancy goods. The recent, tiny, excavation that was undertaken by a team led by Paul Sharman from Orkney College, to enable the rebuild of a section of the island's sheep-dyke (which incidentally offers some small protection to parts of the site) produced all the above objects. These little decorative bone pins and painted pebble are all of the Pictish era. The weaving comb could be any date in the Iron Age. It seems likely that the pebble would have had some magical value. Amongst other things the results, in miniscule, reinforce the impression gained from other more major recent excavations by the Orkney College teams (e.g. Buckan chambered cairn and Knowes of Trotty) that a huge potential for new discoveries remains in sites previously examined by antiquarians.

Dennis Head Lighthouse, North Ronaldsay

The strong tides, stormy winds and fog in Orkney combine with the very low coastlines, shallow waters and reefs of Sanday and North Ronaldsay to make a highly dangerous area for shipping. The risks were even worse for sailing ships. More than 70 ships went down in Orkney waters in the decade 1840 to 1850, many of them off the North Isles. The dangers were first officially recognised after 1740 when North Ronaldsay saw the loss of the Swedish East Indiaman, The Svecia, off its shores. The stone beacon (see page 93) was built in 1789, being only the third such in Scotland. Thomas Smith, the engineer for this beacon was stepfather to Robert the first of the "Lighthouse Stevensons" dynasty. And it was his nephew Alan Stevenson who in 1852 designed the present day lighthouse, left, still the tallest land-based light in Britain. It was built of brick and later painted with white stripes so that it could also be a mark in daylight. Wartime apart, there were never as many wrecks again. This story has another happy ending: the community in North Ronaldsay are now engaged in a project to restore, conserve and sustain the beacon and lighthouse keepers' cottages. NGR HY 783 559.

Lighthouse pier

The shallow shelving beaches made it very awkward to ship in the many tons of bricks and other materials required for the lighthouse buildings. Therefore the first task of the engineers was to build a pier that extends some half a mile out from the land from NGR HY 787 544. This was taken in hand locally.

The Sheep-dyke, North Ronaldsay

This 19th-century wall encircles North Ronaldsay, just above the high tide mark. There was considerable hardship in North Ronaldsay when the kelping boom came to an end. Thirty-two families were forced to leave the island. In the 1830's when the many tiny and annually distributed holdings of run-rigs (strips of cultivable land) were abolished, land was squared off and rented in blocks to fewer people, and the sheepdyke was created. Surplus labour abounded. The idea was to keep cattle inside the dyke, but the sheep were to graze on the shore. Punds (collecting places) and towers (for the sheep to retreat to if cut off by the tide) were created, and the community organised through the Sheep Court for the annual round of maintenance of the sheep and the dyke. Nowadays the dyke is being badly affected by de-population: there are not enough people available or fit enough to keep on repairing it in the face of damage by the sea. The sheep-dyke, and the ancient breed of sheep kept outside it by the islanders, is a huge part of the identity of the island.

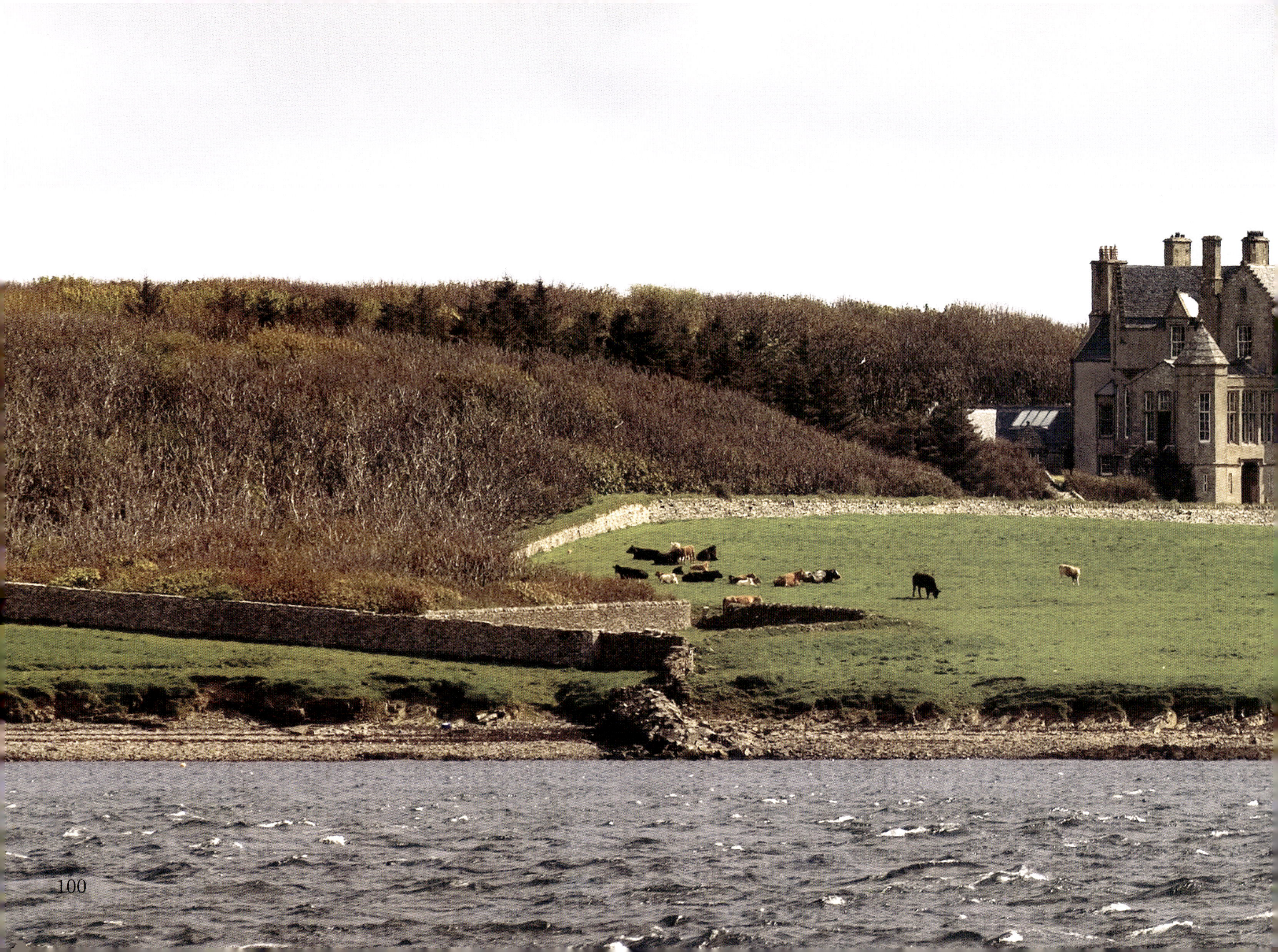

Shapinsay

Odin's Stone, Shapinsay

This is Odin's Stone! At least I believe so. It lies at NGR HY 5064 1914: I give you an eight figure grid reference and measurements so that you can find this very unassuming rock. Lying between the tides, it was used as a marker in the later 18th century to define ownership boundaries in relation to kelping. This may be its only genuine claim to fame. Where the name comes from, or why it is singled out as special, is a bit of a mystery. It measures 2m by 1.4m by 0.5m high.

The Hillock, Shapinsay

This broch is at the north end of Shapinsay (NGR HY 535 228) just beyond the small car park, where a path down to the shore tracks around the right hand side of this grassy mound. The emerging walls can be seen above the distinctive bright orange boulder clay, which forms the drift geology of much of Shapinsay. As yet there is insufficient exposure to be sure what part of the structure we are looking at. Another broch, Burroughston, is in Council guardianship on the northeastern side of Shapinsay. Both are in relatively good order and only just beginning to suffer from erosion.

Human remains are often discovered on broch sites – sometimes in formal cemeteries but often in peculiar circumstances.

Only a small erosion scar is currently exposed. But in this case, a part of a human jaw is coming out of rubble. We do not yet understand the arrangements for the dead of the Iron Age. But it is often the case that body parts are found in brochs e.g. the "piano-playing hands" from Gurness, Evie; or a single articulated leg in the broch ditch at Midhowe, Rousay. Several burials in long cists were discovered in dunes at the other side of the carpark, some 100m to the east.

Galtness and Castle Coastal Batteries, Shapinsay

Begun in 1940 the batteries here were first equipped with a 12 pounder gun in order to provide defence against German e-boats (motor torpedo boats) for Kirkwall harbour, the sites then grew. Located at NGR HY 475 198 these are some of the few sites that are difficult to get to along the shore, and are quite dangerous to try to see from the shore on a rising tide, since the clay cliffs at this point would be difficult to scale. But you get a good view of this site from most of the North Isles ferries (makes the point really, about the location in relation to Kirkwall). So no need to struggle! The search light emplacement is critically undermined.

Broch of Steiro

The broch of Steiro, Shapinsay is pictured with (inset) a great red and yellow sandstone rotary quern eroding from beneath some collapsed rubble.

Some of the North East arc of the outer broch wall survives with an internal platform perhaps representing an upper gallery. On the shore, just above the soft bedrock flagstones have been laid to form a floor. NGR HY 501 163.

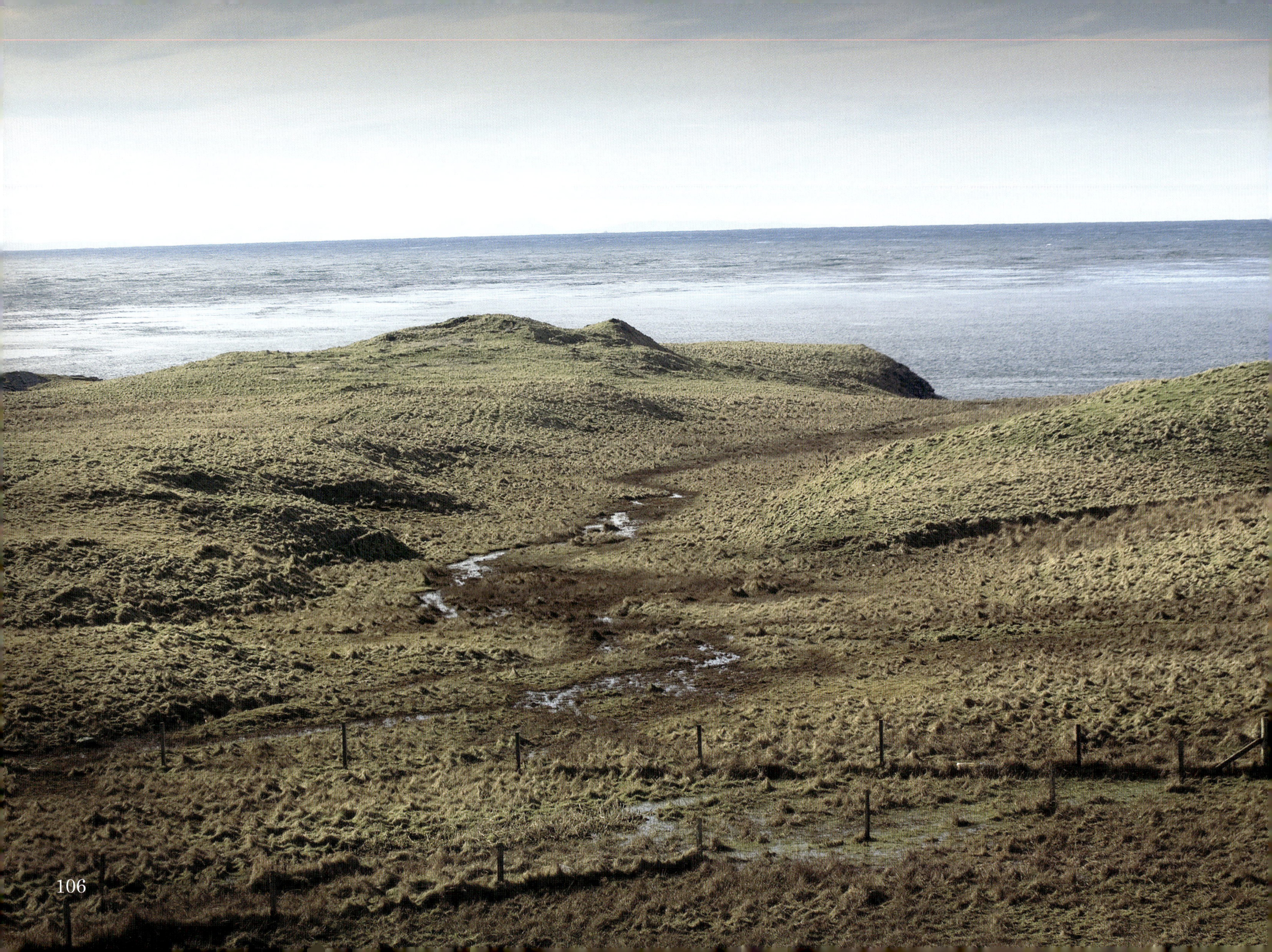

Hoy & Waas

Walls Battery
This battery consists of this twin 6-pounder gun emplacement and three fixed beam search light buildings, plus some magazines and huts. John Guy notes (vol 2 page 65) that there was no overhead cover for the gun. One of the nearby huts was roughly converted for use as a house (as were so many in Orkney after the war) and it was lived in until fairly recently, many of the original fixtures and fittings were retained throughout.
NGR ND 342 910.

Walls Battery

Behind the gun emplacement was the magazine, and crew shelter. The benches in the section at the front were used by the crew in preparing the shells for loading.

Graffiti at Walls Battery

Carefully executed graffiti, recording the names of Sappers (Royal Engineers) of 684 Artisan Workshop, Brown, Lebeter, Warren and Wilkinson – who were stationed here in 1943 and 1944, decorates some of the wartime concrete – a drain outfall, the side of the gun pit and in the field behind. These men were here as soldiers and they left their mark as such.

Brims

"The Skeo" ND 285 879 is relatively undamaged by the sea. This broch and its village sit on a low hillock looking out to sea. An enclosing bank enhances the natural ridge on which it is placed. The erosion on this site seems mainly to be due to burrowing rabbits, though it is always the case that cattle love to rub their itchy heads in earth in the summer time, and to stand dry shod in wet weather, so brochs or burial mounds are often targets for their hoofs and heads.

The Skeo

The Skeo: a midden spills from the interior of the broch mound. The erosion here is being worked on by rabbits. The finds from this midden are typical of finds at a broch site: a sherd of iron age pot and a small trimmed off antler tine. This is probably just a waste piece, but antler was often used for quite fine objects such as hair combs or handles.

The piece of haematite (pictured on Judith Robertson's hand, below) has highly polished or ground faces created by people using the stone for burnishing, or for creating a paste. Haematite-rich natural mineral outcrops can be found in Hoy. This mineral was used in prehistory as a source of iron, and ground finely it produces a bright red pigment.

Prehistoric Landscape near Skipi Geo
The shore lands between Skipi Geo whose name tells all (Skipi is Old Norse for ships, and Geo is a narrow rock bound sea inlet) and The Skeo are a rich coastal landscape including prehistoric sites such as this, and much much more. It is also virtually unsurveyed. These rocks are probably the remains of a chambered cairn.

Crockness Martello Tower

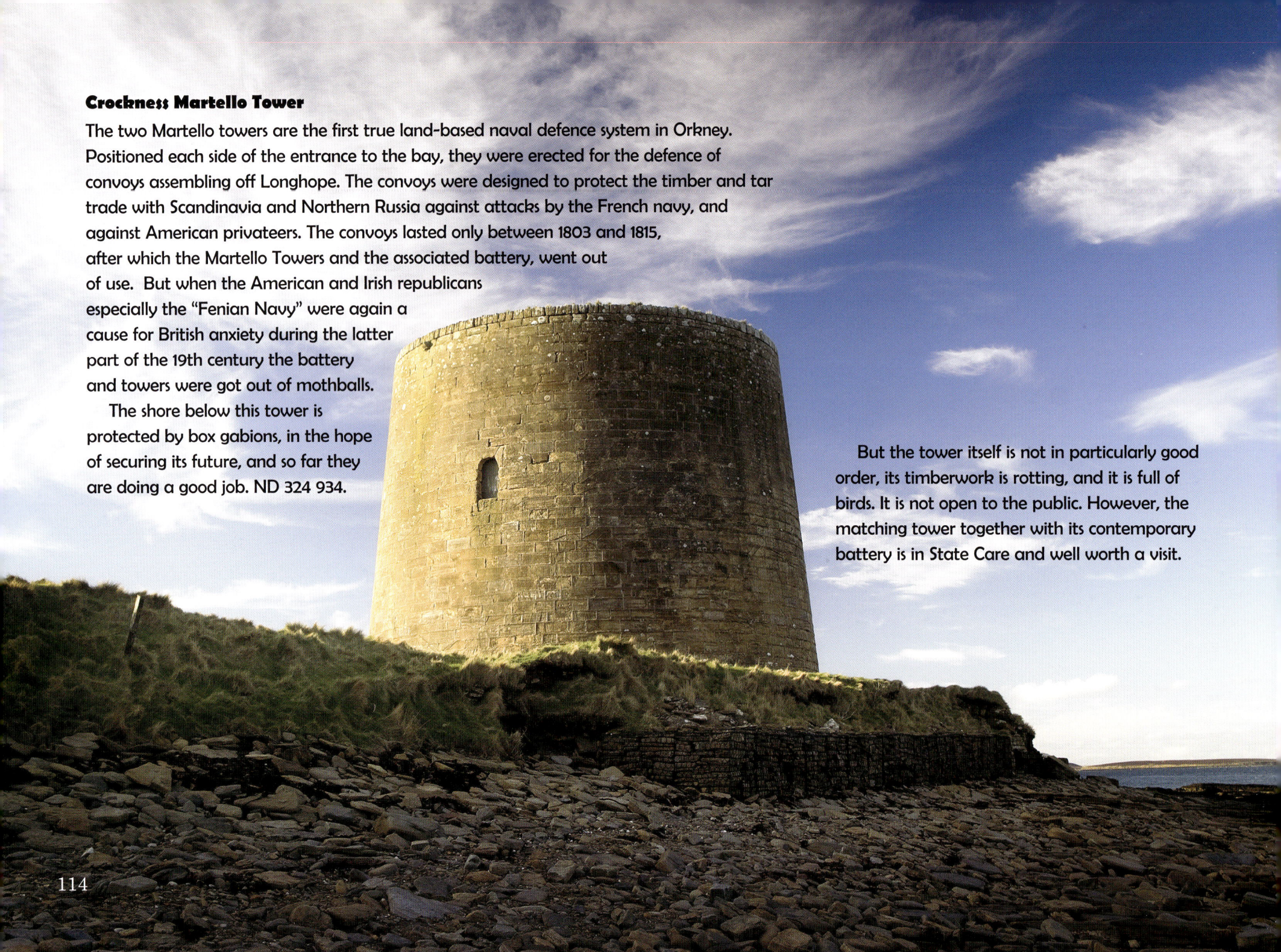

The two Martello towers are the first true land-based naval defence system in Orkney. Positioned each side of the entrance to the bay, they were erected for the defence of convoys assembling off Longhope. The convoys were designed to protect the timber and tar trade with Scandinavia and Northern Russia against attacks by the French navy, and against American privateers. The convoys lasted only between 1803 and 1815, after which the Martello Towers and the associated battery, went out of use. But when the American and Irish republicans especially the "Fenian Navy" were again a cause for British anxiety during the latter part of the 19th century the battery and towers were got out of mothballs.

The shore below this tower is protected by box gabions, in the hope of securing its future, and so far they are doing a good job. ND 324 934.

But the tower itself is not in particularly good order, its timberwork is rotting, and it is full of birds. It is not open to the public. However, the matching tower together with its contemporary battery is in State Care and well worth a visit.

Timeline for coast watchers

Some sites in Orkney span hundreds of years of meaningful activity. Some chambered tombs, for instance, have been a focus in the landscape since they were built. Other sites relate to structures created under very specific political and economic circumstances that came and went in a very short time, like the kelping industry that lasted only some decades. But individual actions of a span of seconds have also left their mark, for instance the place where a few buckets of limpet shells were emptied onto a midden two thousand years ago, is now a feature within a huge farm mound. So, any interpretation and understanding comes with great attention to the detail of each site. But for those unfamiliar with Orcadian archaeology a timeline is provided for a quick round up of what we are talking about.

Conventional wisdom has it that there was no human or mammal here in Orkney during the Ice Age, and that land mammals all came in with people after the retreat of the ice. The following sections deal with typical manifestations of archaeology as it appears on the coast. These are presented in the hope of being a bunch of helpful hints for diagnosing what a particular site might be, when you are only permitted the random views created by erosion.

Mesolithic -about 8,000 years ago:

The first people here to leave much evidence of their presence are the hunter-gatherers of the Mesolithic. The islands were then more wooded, mostly with small trees such as hazel and willow – though many other species were also present. The great shellfish middens that mark the grounds worked seasonally by Mesolithic peoples in other places in Scotland have not yet been discovered in Orkney. Instead evidence of the presence of the people of the time still relies largely upon a few flints found here and there. It is thought that rising sea levels are probably responsible for drowning the evidence of shore-based activity at this time.

Mesolithic flints have most often been found in Neolithic flint scatters or excavations of other kinds of site. For example in 2004 a group were discovered incorporated into the earth of a Bronze Age burial mound at Round Howe, near Mine Howe in Tankerness. Most flints of the Mesolithic are very tiny, smaller than your little fingernail and even a regular hunting camp may gather only a few, so it will be difficult to spot them in the shore banks, unless your eye is first drawn in by another kind of site. Orkney would have looked very different in the Mesolithic, with islands much larger and sea-levels lower but rising fast as the glaciers melted.

Neolithic period c. 3,800 BC to c. 2,000 BC

The Neolithic is characterised by the introduction of farming. The landscape in Orkney changed as farming took hold. Trees were removed. The Neolithic people grew crops such as barley, and kept cattle, sheep and pigs. They also hunted red deer, and fished. We have not found any boats, but it seems clear that some people travelled long distances, and that Orcadian cultural connections in the Neolithic spanned Brittany, Ireland and Southern Britain. The henge sites of the Stones of Stenness and (probably) the Ring of Brodgar, are older than Stonehenge. But the design of interior spaces in houses at Stonehenge and Skara Brae are very similar. In fact, it was the exceptional preservation of the Orcadian Neolithic houses at Skara Brae that allowed for detailed interpretation of the recent discoveries of the remains of wooden houses near Stonehenge.

The stone-built chambered tombs of the period are characterised by differing architectural styles – the oldest type consisting of a long chamber that was subdivided into "stalls" by pairs of large upright flagstones protruding at right angles from the chamber walls. Midhowe, Rousay, is an extremely large example. And in the later period from about 3,000 BC onwards the Maes Howe style chambered tombs were built. These had chambers off the central floor space, set into the fabric of the tomb. Of course there are other types -hybrid types, two-storey chambered tombs, re-designed tombs where a conversion from one style to another has occurred, and so on. The eroded section across the front of the chambered tomb at Tresness, Sanday, shows some of the common characteristics of chambered tombs- a central passage way, and a mound created from concentric single skinned walls back-filled by rubble.

Settlement sites are equally difficult to characterise by the use of architectural style. It used to be thought that rectangular houses (such as Knap of Howar) that were built as individual farmsteads were the earlier form of building. And that by the later Neolithic this was replaced by the buildings with squared interiors, enclosed by circular outer walls, built in villages (such as Skara Brae). But then Barnhouse village near the Stones of Stenness was dug and there amongst the single room dwellings was a double roomed building of incredible longevity. And a giant house that incorporated giant furniture! In 2003 a site below Wideford chambered tomb was excavated and a series of early Neolithic wooden post buildings were discovered – one large and rectilinear, and some others small and round. And since 2007 excavations at the Ness of Brodgar showed us that really we ain't seen nothing yet - for there a huge wall was constructed running across the peninsula, and once again different building shapes are being found. It is true however, that there is a particular very neat style of building, with crisply quarried small stones, laid with precision, that is a marker for the later Neolithic. Otherwise you have to look out for finds, of which there are often many at settlement sites.

Walls exposed in the section are unlikely to carry their own diagnostic characteristics. But a close look at the dark reddish brown soils full of tiny pieces of burnt material – peat ash, flecks of burnt bone, etc that are often associated with the stone work may show flints or pottery in situ. The lower levels at Pool, Sanday still leak large chunks of soggy Grooved Ware Pots – while they are still embedded they look for the most part like gritty chocolate fudge.

The Bronze Age c. 1800 BC to c. 500BC

This is the Cinderella period in Orkney's archaeological literature, but not at all in its landscape: In literature all is dust and ashes. You will find many references to eruptions of the volcano "Hekla" in Iceland, bringing darkness, ash and bad weather to Scotland. Gloomily it is remarked that the peat on the hills grew deep. In reality, there are layers in the peat where fine ash deposits, invisible to the naked eye but possible to make out in the laboratory, mark various Icelandic eruptions and it is true that the weather got noticeably colder and wetter during that millennium, until Orkney had climatic conditions similar to today. Nevertheless in the Bronze Age the population here thrived and expanded up onto the hillsides. Pompeii it was not.

With the usual caveats about the long time periods involved and the inevitable complexities of a variety of burial practices, it is possible to say that burial rites changed in this period from the inhumations of the Neolithic to cremation in the Bronze Age. Orkney's hills and peninsulas were marked by prominent burial mounds, some clustering around the chambered tombs of the past, many others creating new horizons. Antiquarians in the 19th century explored some of the mounds digging the heart out of them, and were disappointed when they found "only cists containing ashes". It is a legacy of that antiquarianism that has led to the received wisdom that in the Bronze Age society underwent a deep recession. But in recent years Jane Downes' Orkney Barrows Project has revolutionised what we can understand from excavating these sites. It is now clear that each cremation was an event requiring a lot of planning and investment from whole families or groups, and culminating in considerable spectacle. The mounds themselves are each very carefully assembled and extensive and complicated barrow cemeteries covering hectares were carefully planned and tidily curated by the people of the Bronze Age. The largest of the mounds at Knowes of Trotty cemetery in Harray contained decorative amber and gold akin to material found in Wessex grave mounds. Here was personal wealth and glamour and an eternal display of it! The stone cists in which remains were interred can be cut into the ground, or built up upon it and then buried beneath a mound of soil or stones, and are easily spotted where they lie in shore sections. (Though they may initially be confused with stone tanks or boxes created as part of settlement sites). Often such burials are in groups. The ashes are often found laid under inverted or broken pots, and may be accompanied by "cramp" which is a form of glassy slag created by fat and the minerals in the peat or turf pyre.

In this period we see a new type of site: Burnt Mounds (ash again, I'm afraid). A Burnt Mound is a pile of broken and heat cracked stone and blackened earth. This results from a water heating activity whereby roasted stones are dropped when hot into water-filled tanks. When the tanks are cleared out, a substantial mound of these red and black shattered stones is created. Burnt mounds are always found near running water or in boggy land. The structures that are involved in the process can be quite complicated and involve water tanks of various shapes and sizes, small buildings, and drains and inlets for controlling running water. Some tanks are large stone cists, with clay packing in the corners to create a waterproof box. Some had lids. (See Meur, Sanday & Warness, Eday) The judges are still out on what they were for: they could be cooking tanks, perhaps for communal feasting, or perhaps saunas. Recently Jane Downes has proposed (pers.comm) that they may be to do with wool or cloth production. The technique of heating water with hot stones can also be found in use in the Iron Age and in the Norse period, but in those periods you find that the burnt stone is part of the settlement debris rather than mounded separately.

Bronze-age houses are drystone structures and have various circular, or rounded forms. Not many have yet been excavated in Orkney. In any case when viewed solely in erosion sections you are not likely to be able to tell Bronze Age settlement from Neolithic or Iron Age without the help of pottery, flints, or other diagnostics.

There is a peculiar form of wall-building that seems to be Bronze Age or Neolithic and which consists of the lower courses being made like a series of boxes.

Iron Age (inc Pictish & Viking Age) c 500BC to c 1000AD

Our Iron Age is like the Scandinavian Iron Age, quite lengthy and not truncated as in England by Roman invasion and colonisation. Of course here, once the Vikings arrived we are really part of the Scandinavian Iron Age, and it is for this reason that Vikings are included in this section.

Iron Age archaeology in Orkney is dominated by the great brochs and their villages. Often these are surrounded by deeply cut ditches, and/or embankments or walls. Sometimes they may be built on or form a peninsular in a loch, or be built into marshy ground. Only rarely are they perched high up on poor ground. It would seem that land management practices associated with the broch builders increased the depths of soil around them; it may actually be their own legacy that has led to the predominance of brochs in what is now good land.

New construction techniques are brought into play in the Iron Age. Cassying is a technique of building flagstones by setting them on edge, packed tightly together like books on a shelf. This is employed as a method of buttressing buildings (see Midhowe broch, Rousay –the broch needed stabilisation at some point during the Iron Age). In later periods this method is often seen employed for building in the intertidal zone, and a modern version made for sea defence can be seen at Midhowe. The sides of ditches are often revetted with a single layer of laid stone walling.

A new architectural understanding of building in storeys comes into play, people are obviously living on the first floor of some brochs, and the first stairs are seen. These can be created like stone ladders, set into walls like stiles, or just made of stone laid on clay. Underground structures are created - deep wells, chambers with steps down, and earth-houses are made. Earth-houses are mostly quite small. Often no more than 1.5m in height they are underground rooms, with flag roofs that are supported on pillars independent from the chamber walls. They are usually associated with dwellings above. They seem to run from the late Bronze Age period right the way through to the post-broch Iron Age.

One of the main features of the Iron Age, as it presents in a coastal section, is the amount of pottery that can be found on the sites, as at Viera Lodge. Sherds of various types of pot from very chunky and rather badly made pots through to the hard-fired pinkish fine pottery of the Pictish (or later Iron Age) period will be leaking from the middens. The use of pottery went out of fashion in the Viking era. Instead steatite for cooking vessels (hot plates and bowls) was brought from Norway or Shetland. This is a fine somewhat shiny and quite soft stone, not found naturally in Orkney. Although steatite is found in other periods, in quantity in a midden it is usually 9th to 12th century AD.

Sometime in this period most of the "farm mounds" of Sanday and other North Isles begin to be formed. These are notable for their huge depth and extent, and large quantities of ashy and sandy soil deposits that interleave with the stony walls of buildings. And somewhere in most of these mounds lie the layers that are "Viking". There are strong hints that Orkney was having some relationship with Scandinavians prior to the arrival of the "Vikings" in the late 8th century AD, but from then on things change radically. Curvy houses go out of use as dwellings, and end up, if they are in use at all, as sheds or dumps. No one is making pretty pink pottery any more, and steatite (soapstone) pots and slabs are used as cooking ware. I would not expect to see the traditional Viking houses (post-built houses, with their skimpy walls made largely of turf) in a coastal section. They would be virtually impossible to spot. There is a requirement to excavate in plan before such a thing can be discovered in a farm mound.

Graves from this period may be almost any shape or type – with people buried in soil in stone cists, that can be either long or short, or in amongst rubble and middens. They can be buried under walls and floors of buildings in use, as well as away from dwellings. Burials may consist of separated body parts! People were also cremated at this time. So it is not possible to recognise an "Iron Age burial" in isolation. In the Viking period we have recognised only inhumations thus far. We are lucky that Vikings who were pagan believed that people could carry their goods with them to their various dwellings after life, so they buried their loved ones with grave goods. Burials in boats were a fashion for the rich. The boat was first dug into the ground surface, and a chamber then made within it by making one or two stone walls and back-filling behind them. Boat graves are marked by the iron rivets that held the planks together. If by a miracle you recognise one of these I want to be the first to know! As Orkney was officially part of the Norwegian kingdom by the 11th century, and Christianity was imposed in 1000AD the term Viking is now being dropped, and I shall refer to the very same people as Norse.

Medieval and modern

It was not long before the simple wooden hall dwellings were out of fashion and by the 12th century Norse buildings are stone and straight walled. Their halls may be subdivided and a house is formed of several rooms (see Quoygrew, Westray). These settlements often have burnt mound material in their middens. At the Brough of Birsay, one of the later and larger houses that has been interpreted as a sauna or bath house was surrounded by a lot of this stuff. The bones of big cod can be seen in abundance in the middens on some sites from the 10 or 11th century and for next two or three hundred years. Some chapels and other high status buildings were lime plastered – with a shelly render. Often stone walls built in the late medieval period, 15th/16th centuries and into modern times have a soft clay infill in the small rubble between the outer faces.

The use of steatite continues for a while but is more or less gone by the 13th century, and a distinctive type of pottery can be found on some sites. Made of a buff fabric, a new style of local pot has many tiny bits of grass impressions on it. Other kinds of rough pottery are also found (very difficult to tell from earlier material) and occasionally a few imports of glazed ware from Scotland or the continent can be seen.

In the 18th and 19th centuries the boom and bust industries of kelp and herring came to Orkney and left their marks on the coastal fringes. Kelp pits are to be found everywhere. They are circular, about a spade's depth and a metre across. The sides of the pit are lined with stones set at a slightly obtuse angle to the flat bottom. The rich kelp lairds built fancy houses in Kirkwall (like the West End Hotel) in which they could spend their winters living the high life. By contrast the many tiny ruins of North Ronaldsay show how the kelp workers themselves fared.

The villages and processing sheds of Whitehall and St Margaret's Hope stand testament to the boom years of herring – the "silver darlings". And tales of walking across harbours dry shod due to the packed numbers of the herring boats, abound. Remnants of the tangle trade can be seen on many of Orkney's shores. Low, loosely constructed drystone or mixed stone and timber racks were created in rows along the shore edge. Here, until very recently, seaweed was collected and draped over the walls to dry before being sold on to industry.

Military sites are to be found all round the coast – from batteries of the 18th and 19th century to the 20th century concrete that is everywhere and which marks the many kinds of installations of the last two world wars. The Scapa Flow wrecks are a focus of the tourism industry, but new survey techniques mean that more wrecks of all kinds are constantly being discovered. One of my favourite wrecks is in Auskerry- a boat that went ashore on rocks with a cargo of teddy bears. Unfortunately together with these wrecks come seamen's graves. Often, washed-up sailors were buried close to where they were found and their graves were not always marked, but being coastal are now prone to erosion. As with all human remains, if you find these graves beginning to surface, they should be reported to the police or the County archaeologist without being touched.

Hopefully this short book will stimulate you to visit at least some of the hundreds of sites currently eroding from the shores of Orkney and undoubtedly you will get a lot from that experience. Sadly, unless there is a change of heart, and governments recognise the potential of our heritage, this generation will be the last to see many of them.

Further Reading and places to get more information:

General:

Downes J et al, 2005 *The Heart of Neolithic Orkney World Heritage Site Research Agenda*. This is published on Historic Scotland's website, it is free to all. This volume is the best background to Orkney's archaeology, as whole. www.historic-scotland.gov.uk/orkneyresearch

Berry, RJ 1985 *The Natural History of Orkney*, London

Fenton, A 1978 *The Northern Isles: Orkney and Shetland*, Edinburgh

Ritchie, A 1995 *Prehistoric Orkney*, London (If you have no previous knowledge of Orcadian archaeology start with this one, and Thomson, 2001, below)

Thomson, W P L 2001 *A New History of Orkney*, Edinburgh

Royal Commission on Ancient and Historical Monuments Scotland: The national database website CANMORE is easily searchable for information and detailed references to each site listed in this book. www.rchahms.gov.uk

Proceedings of the Society of Antiquaries of Scotland. The main journal of publication for all archaeological articles in Scotland, since the 19th century. Except for the most recent volumes it is on-line, including illustrations. http://ads.ahds.ac.uk/catalogue/ARCHway/

The Sites and Monuments Record in Orkney holds a lot of unpublished material, maps, post war aerial photos etc., contact Julie Gibson at the archaeology department at Orkney College for an appointment. Julie.gibson@orkney.uhi.ac.uk

The Orkney Room in the Orkney Library holds an exceptional collection of material

www.scapetrust.org is the website for Scottish Coastal Archaeology and the Problem of Erosion.. The only place really for the wider Scottish perspective, see Dawson, 2003 below.

A Scottish Archaeological Research Framework (Scarf) http://www.scottishheritagehub.com/content/welcome Just launched, May 2012.

Period or topic specific:

Anderson, J 1873 *The Orkneyinga Saga*, Edinburgh or choose the Penguin version by Palsson and Edwards.

Armit, I *Towers in the North: the Brochs of Scotland*, Stroud

Ballin Smith, B and Banks, I (eds) 2002 *In the Shadow of the Brochs: the Iron Age in Scotland*

Barclay ,G J (ed) 1997 State-Funded *"Rescue"Archaeology in Scotland*, Edinburgh. Historic Scotland Ancient Monument Divison Occasional Paper 2. This is old but is still their most recent word on the topic. State funds remain as they were – flatlined.

James Barrett has published many papers on the medieval fish trade, and interim reports on the sites he has excavated at Quoygrew and the Brough of Deerness. Google them.

Burgher,L 1991 *Orkney, An Illustrated Architectural Guide*, Rutland

Buteaux, S 1997 *Settlements at Skaill, Deerness, Orkney – Excavations by Peter Gelling of the Prehistoric, Pictish Viking and Later Periods,1963-1981*. Includes many illustrations of pottery and other items.

Dawson, S and Wickham-Jones, C R *The Rising Tide: Submerged Landscape of Orkney*. <http://www.abdn.ac.uk/staffpages/uploads/arc007/ various reports 2004-2011

Further reading

Dockrill, S J 2007 *Investigations in Sanday, Orkney Vol 2: Tofts Ness, Sanday. An island landscape through 3,000 years of prehistory*, Kirkwall

Downes J and Lamb, RG 2000 *Prehistoric Houses at Sumburgh in Shetland*, Oxford. (Bronze Age houses)

Downes, J and Ritchie, A (eds) 2003 *Sea Change: Orkney and Northern Europe in the later Iron Age AD 300-800*, Balgavies

Ferguson, D M 1985 *The Wrecks of Scapa Flow*

Hewison, W S 1995 *Scapa Flow in War and Peace*, Kirkwall

Hunter, J with Bond J M and Smith A N 2007 *Investigations in Sanday,Orkney vol 1: Excavations at Pool, Sanday A multiperiod settlement from the Neolithic to Late Norse times*

Low,C E 1998 *St Boniface Church, Orkney Coastal Erosion and Archaeological Assessment*. More than a site report – a fine experiment in an innovative excavation technique explained.

Marwick, H 1952 *Orkney Farm Names*, Kirkwall. (He also published many other placename articles, over nearly 50 years)

Moore, H and Wilson G, *Report on a Coastal Zone Assessment of Orkney 1997, Burray, Flotta, Graemsay, Hoy and South Ronaldsay; 1998, Westray, Papa Westray, South Mainland; 1999 Sanday, North Ronaldsay*, Historic Scotland. (may be consulted in SMR)

Moore, H and Wilson G 2011 *Shifting Sands Links of Noltland, Westray: Interim Report on Neolithic and Bronze Age Excavations, 2007-9* Historic Scotland Archaeology Report no 4

Owen, O and Dalland, M 1999 Scar, *A Viking Boat Burial on Sanday, Orkney*, East Linton

Richards, C (ed) *Dwelling Among the Monuments. Excavations at Barnhouse, and Maeshowe, Orkney*. Cambridge

Ritchie, A (ed) 2000 *Neolithic Orkney in its European Context*

Wickham-Jones, C R 1994 *Scotland's First Settlers*, London

Tom Dawson (ed) 2003 *Coastal Archaeology and Erosion in Scotland - Conference Proceedings*. This volume covers a wide variety of topics including predictions for sea-level change. Free to download. www.historic-scotland.gov.uk/coastalconferenceproceedings

Points to note:

Where archaeology has been studied, surveyed or excavated in the last decade, nearly all sponsorship has been by Orkney Islands Council and Historic Scotland regularly has contributed. The archaeologists (professional and volunteer) and their institutions themselves contribute time and expertise. No projects could have taken place successfully without the huge support, put in year after year, by the communities in which the archaeologists are working. Each part of that partnership is vital to any study taking place. The Orkney Archaeological Society have been mining every pocket in Orkney and beyond for cash to help with the coastal erosion crisis. In recent years the Heritage Lottery Fund has provided funds for Shorewatch and the projects at Quoygrew and North Ronaldsay lighthouses. All contributions have been, and will be, gratefully received!

The main point of contact for reporting eroding archaeology in Orkney is the Archaeology Department Orkney College, Kirkwall. KW15 1LX. Tel +44 (0)1856 569341 and Tankerness House Museum, Kirkwall: Tel 01856 873535.
Email julie.gibson@orkney.uhi.ac.uk.

Orkney Archaeology Society

The Orkney Archaeology Society (OAS) is very pleased to be able to support the publication of *Rising Tides Revisited*. OAS has been supporting archaeology in Orkney since 2008 and prior to that, in our previous incarnation, as The Friends of Orkney Archaeological Trust (FOAT).

The Society offers practical and financial support to archaeologists in Orkney through small grants towards fieldwork and post excavation work. OAS members get involved in excavations and helping out at our fundraising shop – found at OAS events and major OAS supported digs across the county. OAS also promotes Orkney archaeology through education and raising public awareness with walks, talks, events and publications. All this requires funds and fundraising is another important part of the work of the Society.

The late Daphne Lorimer was a founding member of FOAT and her enthusiasm and legacy live on as the Daphne Lorimer Bursary Fund which contributes towards the fees for a student attending the MA in Archaeology Practice at Orkney College each year. This enables a student, who would otherwise not be able to attend, to contribute to the wider understanding of archaeology in Orkney through their research. To support this, OAS undertakes a major fundraising event each year to pay for this important bursary. This year we have pledged the profits from *Rising Tides Revisited* to the Daphne Lorimer Bursary Fund. The Orkney Archaeology Society would like to say a very big thank you to Frank Bradford and Julie Gibson, *Rising Tides Revisited* photographer and author, for their generosity and time in revising the original Rising Tides book and allowing OAS to use the funds raised through the book sales to go towards the Daphne Lorimer Fund. We would also like to say thank you to our sponsors who contributed to the costs of producing and publishing this new edition. And finally, thank you to all our OAS members and the people who buy this book. By purchasing this book you are making a very real contribution to archaeology education and research in Orkney. Thank you.

Kind sponsors of Rising Tides Revisited: Various anonymous donors; Anne Marie Ward; Breckness Estate, Skaill House, Sandwick; Ella Henderson; Fursbreck Pottery, Harray; Jean A Thomson in memory of Jessie Simpson; Jeremy Baster; Jolly's, Kirkwall; Keith and Ruth Brown; The Mollie Lind Charitable Trust, Drever and Heddle, Kirkwall; Tomb of the Eagles, South Ronaldsay; Trudi Terry and Irene Dickerman, Virginia, USA.

Find out more or join the Orkney Archaeology Society at http://orkneyarchaeologysociety.org.uk